HEBREW & GREEK STUDY DELIVERANCE MANUAL

FOREWORD BY **APOSTLE LARRY PRATCHER, JR.**

BLOODLINE
SPIRITUAL
DNA

IDENTITY

Yeshua Ha-Mashiach

Ambassadors 4 Christ

EVANGELIST DELMELODIA TIPTON

authorHOUSE®

AuthorHouse™
1663 Liberty Drive
Bloomington, IN 47403
www.authorhouse.com
Phone: 1 (800) 839-8640

Logo design by Rasheda Davis
www.bvpllc.biz

Edited by Rhonda Wilson

Published by AuthorHouse   08/01/2017

ISBN: 978-1-5246-5620-1 (sc)
ISBN: 978-1-5246-5618-8 (hc)
ISBN: 978-1-5246-5619-5 (e)

Library of Congress Control Number: 2017900004

Print information available on the last page.

DEDICATION & ACKNOWLEDGEMENT

ALL GLORY, PRAISE AND HONOR I GIVE UNTO YAHWEH,
YESHUA, AND RUACH HAKODESH FOR THE PRIVILEGE
AND OPPORTUNITY TO TOUCH THE NATIONS WITH
GRACE, TRUTH, WORD OF KNOWLEDGE AND WORD
OF WISDOM THROUGH THE COUNSEL OF HOLINESS.
THIS WORK IS DEDICATED TO THE ADVANCEMENT
OF THE KINGDOM OF YAHWEH IN YESHUA
THROUGH EARTHLY VESSELS AS IT IS IN HEAVEN.

BE THY GLORIED HEAVENLY FATHER IN THIS WORK.

ENDORSEMENTS

Bloodline Spiritual DNA is a powerful and riveting book! Enormously helpful to those who are seeking to learn more about Yahweh and their identity. If you are yearning for a deeper knowledge of the union between God and His children- this book will be informative and helpful in your quest.

_Mr. and Mrs. Roland Wilson

Evangelist Delmelodia Tipton is an inspiring writer with an anointing to set the captives free. We have known Evangelist Tipton for several years and have experienced the fire of God upon her life to loose souls from the kingdom of darkness. In this book, Spiritual DNA, you will be blessed to identify the openings that Satan has used to keep souls and families in bondage through generational curses. You will also learn strategies to break bloodline cycles in your life, to set you and the next generation on a path that leads to total freedom. This study manual is a deliverance tool for believers who are willing to embrace the instructions written in the Word of God. And to see yourself and the next generation free from demonic, mental and emotional torment. It is our prayer to encourage each reader to become serious about your walk before the eternal King that your name may be written in the Book of Life. The ingredients written within this book, along with the Word of God, is needed to help us (the Body of Christ) to be free from unclean spirits and to live a life pleasing to our Father above. May the work of the Lord cause us to be blessed and cleaned by the blood of Yeshua (Jesus) and the Ruach HaKodesh (Holy Spirit)! A greater breakthrough is headed your way.

_Minister Terence & Intercessor/Author Rasheda Davis
The School of Intercession
www.soipropheticwatch.com

ABOUT THE AUTHOR

Delmelodia Tipton is a woman of faith, wife, mother, entrepreneur and the author of two powerful Spirit filled inspired study manuals impacted with divine knowledge, revelation and wisdom from the LORD to impart and deepen spiritual understanding for navigating in this world as sons and daughters of Yahweh in Christ Jesus. Evangelist Tipton is founder/ host of AMBASSADORS 4CHRIST APOSTOLIC BROADCAST MINISTRY where she and other Ambassadors for Christ flow in the apostolic, revelatory teachings and demonstrations of Christ. Delmelodia Tipton believes the apostolic ministry of Christ is still relevant today for the purpose of bringing the Church to a state of active maturity in the spiritual and natural blessings of Yahweh. She teaches the Hebraic origin of the Christian faith that unfolds the mystery and purpose of the LORD for His body today. Delmelodia

Tipton actively believes in the power of intercession and the power of deliverance. She discovered and accepted her mantle on her life in 2004 under the leadership of Apostle Larry and Prophetess Iliana Pratcher. Tipton has served over the years faithfully in outreach ministry in the capacity of evangelizing in the mission field of street ministry, feeding the homeless, women's prison ministry and the nursing home ministry for several years. Tipton served as youth director for six years (Warriors In Christ Youth Ministry) and dance leader of Unity of Praise Worship Ministry. Visit the website for ministry information, broadcasts, booking, prayer, books and custom t-shirts ordering @ www.ambassaduer4christ.net.

FOREWORD

It is with great honor and respect that I offer you this foreword for this great resource. I have had the privilege and honor to witness the growth and spiritual maturity of Evangelist Delmelodia Tipton first-hand. Over the past 12 years she has served as a youth leader, intercessor and part of the ministerial ministry and now the author of her second book. Holy Spirit has truly been nurturing and cultivating this woman of God. This biblically sound resource about the Bloodline is evidence of a person that has been through her share of trials and tribulations, but now she has taken the time to take notes of the spiritual nuggets the Lord has downloaded into her for such a time as this. Evangelist Tipton has been well trained by Ruach HaKodesh (Holy Spirit) in trusting in the Lord to walk with you in the hardest times of life. This book deals with many serious topics from the dissecting of the seed, spiritual genes, kingdom mindset and the Divine Nature given to us from the Father. It is my belief that after reading this epistle, you will have more understanding of the details of the nature of the Bloodline and many other spiritual insights. This epistle will bless your life. I declare that you will be blessed due to the many tears, prayers and the dedication it took to write an end-time epistle. Enjoy & Receive!

_Apostle Larry Pratcher,Jr.
TBOC (The Body of Christ) MINISTRY

CONTENTS

INTRODUCTION

It is very important for us to be absolute in the understanding of our uniqueness in Jesus Christ as sons and daughters of Yahweh. Our physical individuality is what is given in the physical birth, but the Body of Christ has virtue of supreme worth within that is the cloak of our true divine identity. This supernatural DNA isn't based on the color of your skin, how much money you have or do not have, age, who you're related to, connected to, race or education status. It's not based on the damnable names or unwholesome words that may have been spoken against you that defines the essence of who you really are. It's not defined by how low you may have fallen, how long you have been there or what heights you have or have not reach. It's not based on your quality of living. Our souls which is the absorption of His Breath was permeated with Yahweh Elohim's essence and glory from the beginning. When we understand and receive the magnitude in knowing our complete true identity as sons of GOD, adopted in the family of Yahweh, it shifts the total perception toward the predestined path that is purposed for every blood washed, Spirit-filled, born again believer. The DNA re-establishes agreement, thought, kingship, behavior, reaction and destiny forever and ever. What was lost is recovered and restored through Yeshua.

There are different types of outside entities that can play a part in shaping one's identity, but only the one true GOD can recreate the new and cancel out the old. The personal issues that exist far too often with one's personal identity come from within. Although personal identity is targeted by outward influences those influences target the imagination. The imagination projects an image in the mind with a choice to receive or reject, react or refuse that which came from the outside. Thoughts are seeds planted for the purpose of revealing that thought. Identity in Christ transforms our thought system; which in return orders our steps. Identity in Christ as a son of Yahweh empowers the believer to overthrow every lie, every curse and darkness with its desires to hold you captive. In Christ we can do all things, but without Christ we cannot do anything because the knowledge and power of the DNA is from heaven above not earth below. The Power of knowing, recognizing and living through the Spirit infuses the believer with divine power to throwback that which is contrary to one's true identity in Christ Jesus. Therefore, rebuke the lies and lay hold of the Kingdom of Yahweh by force in the name of Yeshua HaMashiach (Jesus Christ).

During the process of writing my first book, <u>In the Midst of the Storm There Is Purpose</u>, the Spirit of the LORD whispered His thought into my spirit for the title and purpose of this second book, <u>Bloodline, Spiritual DNA</u>. Yahweh's divine purpose by His Spirit is to bring wisdom and revelation concerning spiritual matters of the mind, the heart, the image, to set at liberty the captives, to break death cycles, wrong persuasion, uproot the seed of wrong thinking, cancel wrong motives, to unleash mass deliverance, to produce liberation of new-life empowerment and to re-establish creative divine order through His Divine Nature (DNA) to the spirit, soul and body. I was prompt to research even further on genes, genetics and chromosomes due to the experience of my first born who was diagnosed with Wolf-Hirsh Syndrome II. Recalling the Word of GOD that there is nothing new under the sun which means that everything that exist has an origin, even though under another name and that the SON is an originator. The Spirit of the LORD enlightened me with a breath of revelation and knowledge of how everything spawned in the physical realm from a spiritual genetic code. The revelation Ruach HaKodesh provided paints a picture to illustrate to the senses of the imagination.

This manual unloads the insight behind the visual elements of the seed, bloodline and the genetics of the two trees in the midst of the Garden of Eden and how they supernaturally and naturally relate to humanity in chronos and kairos in the universe according to scripture. Understanding and implementing your identity in Christ changes the way we think, our emotions and our actions. Who are you really? How do you know that? What is your nature? Who told you that? Where did it originate from? What is your identity position? Who told you that? Why do you behave as you do? What has dominion over you? Why? How? Who is the source of your being? What does it mean to reign in dominion? In most cases situations exist because they have been given legal entry and birth through the mind and soul. The Ekklesia thoughts and actions are commanded to be in alignment with the Ruach of Yahweh-Elohim which is the reflection of sonship. The antidote for complete healing is in the DNA code of the Seed of Righteousness.

John 17:24

Father, I will that they also, whom thou hast given me, be with me where I am; that they may behold my glory, which thou hast given me: for thou loved me before the foundation of the world.

Ephesians 1:4

According as He (Yeshua) hath chosen us in him before
the foundation of the world, that we should be holy
and without blame before him (Yeshua) in love.

Lord let the blind eyes be opened, bring out the
prisoners from prison and those that sit in
darkness out of the prison house. Let new
things be declared in my life and
let them spring forth.

Isaiah 42:7, 9

1

SEED

When the Spirit of GOD gives birth He sustains what is birth through His DNA by the power of His Breathe. The Ekklesia *(the Body of Christ)* is a treasure of magnificent value and is the investment of Yahweh-Elohim. You are the apple of His eye. You are His plan, His purpose and His thought manifested with great potential significance. He invested His image in dust *(us)* through SEED form. Blood bought believers aren't just human, but as jars of clay we're "to be" filled continuously with the sacred prosperity of heaven. Divinely restored believers are earthly vessels with a supernatural treasure that makes it clear that our great source of power is from Elohim and not from ourselves *{2 Corinthians 4:7}*. Elohim is the Guarantor, Provider, Sower and Strong One of this SEED investment. As your understanding is developed of what, when, where, why and how seed performs it will unlock the spiritual mystery of binding and loosing, spiritual deposits, planting, reaping, cultivating and weeding out. If GOD did not plant it, it is not from Him and what is not of Him must be rooted out through the process of reciprocation. Without a seed there cannot be a harvest. Everything originates genetically from a seed. When there is a need a seed is sown first and then it must die to reach its full potential of purpose. Just as it is with the performance of a physical seed likewise is the performance of a spiritual seed which relates directly to us as believers and our spirituality. A seed is sown for the purpose of yielding a return. At Yahweh's appointed time, He casted forth His plan that was **Already** predestined by casting His SEED. Although that which the LORD casted was immaterial first, it materialized into the physical realm. He thought a thing and His thoughts in the form of SEED went forth and His thoughts manifested; the SEED of authority. Yahweh's method of creating by His SEED is the divine **principle** that is used in the physical and spiritual realm today. This is a principle that works for anyone that works it and for this reason was the Son of GOD revealed to destroy the works of the evil one *{1 John 3:8}*.

The incorruptible SEED is the bloodline carrier of the DNA-GOD Gene. The SEED, Yeshua HaMashiach, substituted Himself for the world by putting on our garments of filth, shame, sorrow and imperfection to show the royal way. And the incorruptible SEED in exchange still re-establishes many as kinsmen through His righteous government. Those which are planted for the Glory of the LORD shall grow into trees of righteousness and for as many as are led by the Spirit of GOD, these are the sons of GOD through the glory and power of the incorruptible SEED *{Psalms 92:12; Romans 8:14}*. That which is planted of the LORD is sustained by the Tree of Life to produce in its season, overcome and to be fruitful without ceasing.

Therefore, whatever stands in ones way to block is overcome only by the authority of the SEED activation within. Prevailing in abundance like the olive tree for the Lord's display of promise, honor and glory. Like a tree planted by the streams of living water the LORD provides His crown of beauty, garment of purity, protection, strength, love and the flourishing way that leads to spiritual and natural development and prosperity *{3 John v2}*. The **substance** of the incorruptible SEED is deposited in the new creature. In the natural sphere when a seed is sown, planted and penetrated into the soil it takes root and germinate for the purpose of producing wholesome healthy fruit of its own nature, yielding forth a wholesome harvest. As a seed is being cultivated by the true Light source it will begin to respond and react to the Light from which it is knitted to; **the two become one**. This electrical charge jump starts, molds, structures and draws out the inner substance successfully that will bring continual transformation and glory as long as the soil is rich and pliable. This is the growth process in relation to the law of reciprocity. The seed gives and the soil broadcast acceptance through exchange. The seed recognizes that the inward substance is the force that reveals its greatness, purpose, calling, assignments and anointing. Now revert those attributes and apply them personally. Believers are the vessels that the SEED of Righteousness makes its deposit in for the process of uprooting, rooting, budding and blossoming; establishing the Kingdom of Yahweh within. No matter what the atmospheric temperature maybe the incorruptible SEED supernaturally has the thought to withstand outer spiritual interference that tempts to dislodge its root system when grounded. However, the proper environment, surrounding or atmosphere for the SEED to be active is dependent upon you personally. The enemy will always attempt to sow his seed of thorns, weed and bristles in any soil, especially targeting babes in the LORD that aren't nurtured and grounded. In all seasons the soil has to be nurtured, watered, protected and cared for by you and GOD will provide the increase *{Hosea 14:7-9}*. The increase can manifest in unlimited ways, such as, self-control, divine strength, meekness, humility, peace of mind, divine knowledge and open doors. GOD is the owner of the spiritual house and the righteous SEED contains the blueprint for the new spiritual house that is not made with man hands. Believers are stewards that are to broadcast good stewardship over their new house through willingness and submission. Yahweh's SEED structures sonship from within and cultivation of the soul "to be"*(intimately)* **one** in marriage, one in blood, **one** in thought, **one** in Word, **one** in Spirit, **one** in mind and creating actions of **oneness**. The SEED is the essence of Jehovah *(Yahweh)* and the grace to our physical and resurrected life in this world in Yeshua *(Jesus)*. The SEED possesses ABBA's glory and identity and is the supernatural source of spiritual fertility. The SEED sacrificed itself in order to bring forth seeds of righteousness. Yeshua, the SEED of Righteousness, compares Himself to a seed of wheat that must die first before bearing more seed *{John 12:23-25}*. The SEED points to the abundant life hidden in Christ: Salvation, the Cross of Cavalry, Eternity, Victory over the sin nature's corruption from ADAM and Victory over death and disease. Through the Cross we die to the sin nature. We crucify and bury the old nature's marred soulish identity and confused mindset and we are raised to live and walk in Christ our divine nature and true identity. ***The Word of GOD declares in 1 Peter 1:23 Being born again, not of corruptible seed, but of the incorruptible, by the Word of GOD, which lives and abides forever.*** Christ complete sacrifice *(death, burial, resurrection and glorification)* gave spiritual birth to bring forth heirs of GOD that we may share in His Glory as sons of GOD *{1 John 3; 5, 9}*.

The penetration of the SEED and its death causes a biochemical reaction. Just as it is when a male sperm -seed- comes into contact with a fertile egg there will be a chemical reaction from the two cells uniting them as one resulting in fertilization, multiplication and oneness. The SEED supernatural ability is to produce life, create the new and to destroy. The SEED authority and power supernaturally stops unwarranted life patterns and cycles. When something reoccurs or continues to repeat itself again and again and again that is called a cycle; the recurring of an episode negative or positive, good or bad is the evidence of the dominion of that particular seed of thought. If the seed is foul the fruit will be diseased, tainted and unfit. However, the holy SEED is the divine government of Yahweh-Elohim creative order in all of creation providing the DNA imprint in order to be fit for the master's heritage.

Yahweh *(GOD)* who is all Spirit by His Ruach co-labored with His Eternal WORD -SEED- created and manifested what is seen and what is unseen in the universe before the casting of His SEED before the foundation of the world. Yahweh-Elohim *(the Father, the Son, Holy Spirit)* revealed the essence of His self-existence nature through the agreement of covenant with Himself by His SEED. The word seed which relates to the spiritual laws of the Kingdom of Yahweh is mentioned throughout the Bible from Genesis to Revelation numerous of times. Understanding the power to govern and the characteristics of the DNA *(divine nature)* GOD SEED empowers the believer to reign in the supernatural by mastering any sin, temptation, corrupt emotions and thoughts and to live in true prosperity and harmony. The Eternal WORD or SEED carries heavy weight in the provision of Yahweh-Elohim with no internal or external hindrances. Nothing that has happened or is happening has taken the Godhead *(triune*

God-Elohim) by surprise. Elohim's provision surpasses all worlds, time and flesh. Yahweh is outside of time, any other power and He sees afar off the appointing seasons that are to manifest in their due time. The future of the SEED "In the Beginning" prophetically speaks of the King, His Kingdom and His royal genos *(race, kin),* a representation of the Father's internal reality of Glory, Spirit Dominance, Spirit Power, Success, Kinship and Existence.

- *The Word of GOD declares in John 1:3 All things were made by him (Yeshua); and without him (Yeshua-Jesus) was not any thing made that was made.*

- *The Word of GOD declares in Colossians 1:16 For by him (Jesus-Yeshua) were all things created, that are in heaven, and that are in earth, visible and invisible, whether they be thrones, or dominions, or principalities, or powers: all things were created by him, and for him.*

The Institution known as the Ekklesia, Church, *(the spiritual body of community of believers who are called out of darkness into the light)* was already predestined in Christ to reign and rule in dominion and abundance in the earth as the sons of Yahweh. The phrase sons of GOD refers to neither male nor female *{Galatians 3:28}*, because we are born of Yahweh from above; believers are spiritual beings in an earthly suit. Sons *(Hebrew word ben, bane)* born of Elohim, the children of Elohim, who are spirit-elohim. Spirit begot spiritual children through **one** holy incorruptible SEED. Who we are to become is in Yeshua! What we are to be is in Yeshua! And the map to obtaining our destiny is in Yeshua as we walk *(live)* by the Ruach *(Spirit)*! We loose ground and become mislead and corrupt without Yeshua! There is no other authority or Promise without Yeshua! There is no other divine knowledge outside of Yeshua! There is no other power to overcome in this world without Yeshua! There is no true salvation or deliverance or identity without Yeshua, the Son of the living GOD! There is no heavenly eternal bliss without reigning through, by, under and in Yeshua! *The Word of GOD declares in Galatians 4:6-7 Because you are sons, God has sent forth the Spirit of His Son into our hearts, crying, ABBA! Father! Therefore, you are no longer a slave, but a son; if a son, then an heir of YHWH through Christ.*

Hebrew term for Dominion
Memshalah: authority, power to govern, rule, domain

Greek word for Seed
Sperma: seed, seminal
Hebrew terms for Seed
Zara: plant, give birth, scatter / Zera: intercourse, posterity

- *The Word of GOD declares in Genesis 2:9, 15-17 And out of the ground made the Lord God to grow every tree that is pleasant to sight, and good for food; and the tree of life also in the midst of the garden, and the tree of knowledge of good and evil. And the LORD God took the man and put him into the Garden of Eden to dress it and to keep it. And*

the LORD God commanded the man, saying of every tree of the garden thou may freely eat: But of the tree of knowledge of good and evil, thou shall not eat of it: for in that day that thou shall eat therefore thou shall surely die.

Elohim forethought what was in the dust of the ground in which He formed ADAM and with that same divine wisdom governed ADAM to abide under an open heaven and in His Presence as an immortal being, a king and a god *(elohim)* in that divine appointed time. Although Elohim foreknew Adam *(Eve)* needed to know, recognize and be able to make a conscious choice to live or die, to obey or disobey, attempt to serve two masters *(serve one and hate the other)* or abide by the Spirit of wisdom that was already given to them. All of this we understand in part, but ADAM did not recognize the power of the diseased seed of Satan; its persuasion through his wife, the power of choice or the mind of fallen nature. Eve's temptation grew and expanded through the mind's desire, weakness, carousing and delusion resulting in spiritual drunkenness from omitting the Law of Wisdom and being in the wrong atmosphere that presented a wicked presence. There is a danger and weakness when a believer neglects the wisdom of the LORD; consumed by the inner desires to indulge. Delighting in the wrong atmosphere rises from affections within to gratify the temptations of the flesh. We are instructed to be alert and pray so our physical weaknesses and gratifications will not overpower our will to obey the LORD; and our minds will not be weighed down with the anxieties of life and spiritual drunkenness so that day will not come upon us suddenly like a trap *{Luke 21:34}*. Holy Spirit opens spiritual ears to hear and spiritual eyes to see. The Body of Christ must remain spiritual vigilant, ready to deny the fallen nature, counterattack the bait of the enemy and be empowered to overcome the evil one *{1Peter 5:8}*.

Prayer

Heavenly Father in the Name of Yeshua (Jesus) as I Humble Myself to Study Your Holy WORD, I Ask that You Increase my Spiritual Awareness, Open My Spiritual Eyes and Ears So I will Not Be Deceived Or Walk in Deception. Speak to My Heart and Direct My Footsteps LORD in the Path that I Shall Go. Father I Give You my Desires and Affections and Ask You to Sanctify Them and Make Me Whole For I Am Created In Your Image. I'm Yours LORD.

Amen.

It is recorded as 600 years of dominancy from the royal house of King David that the Hand of the LORD brought forth a righteous Branch out of the stump of Jesse *(father of David)* *{Isaiah 10:33-34}*. Every tree is known by the type of fruit that it produces. Every branch is sustained and nurtured by the roots of that tree from the source of that Seed. The seed that births that tree holds its complete garment, distinction, nature, mark and purpose. The holy SEED is the transmitting GOD-gene carrier of His **fullness**. Yahweh is GOD of abundance not lack. The Spirit of abundance flows from the source of abundance; the spirit of deficiency flows from its source. The SEED of Righteousness -DNA- is the power key to release the Father's inheritance of blessings, glory, Spirit, wealth, dominion and advancement.

Yahweh uses patterns to lay bare His Divine Glory, Wisdom, Power and Awesomeness. Therefore, we pattern after new life by the Spirit's blueprint. The flesh is weak, but the Spirit is willing *{Matthew 26:41}*. As sons of Yahweh in Christ Jesus, we are commanded to speak life and not death. Speaking forth is an expression of the DNA GOD-gene we have. The sound of the Word of GOD being cast -Seed- is like a vibration in the sphere created to govern the atmosphere. I repeat, "The SOUND of the WORD OF GOD, SEED Being Spoken Is Like VIBRATION in the spirit realm TO GOVERN THE ATMOSPHERE ACCORDING TO THE FATHER'S WILL." People of FAITH, we have a supernatural powerful gift within us that is beyond the wisdom of men and creation. The law of vibration extends from God's universe to the universe of the worlds. The Spirit of GOD hovered over the waters by His decree changing chaos *{Genesis 1:2}*. Our words have power to create, change, hurt, heal, build, direct, persuade or destroy; we are warned that life and death is in the power of the tongue and those who love it will eat its fruit *{Proverbs 18:21}*. Therefore, as a benefit of being a son we have the power to cancel things in the atmosphere by the power of the **WORD of GOD** from a pure heart and clean hands. We have power to speak those things that are not as though they were because of faith and by faith we are declaring what ABBA has already declared to be so by **His Spirit**. The believing believer has authority to speak forth the mystery of heaven into the earth; Thy Kingdom Come, Thy Will Be Done On Earth, As It Is In Heaven *{Matthew 6:10}*. Speaking the WORD of GOD which is "the SEED" is a Law of the Kingdom; divinely spoken through thought for the purpose of creating *{Luke 8:11}*. And what one speaks is often a reflection of their character, heart, thoughts and imagination or emptiness or fullness. Let's get full of the WORD for Yahweh's name sake. When a seed is planted in the ground it sprouts downward for the purpose of fortification. Words are seed and words are spirit; when they are released into the atmosphere they can take root in the mind. When your mind is grounded in the WORD of GOD it will call for reflections and inspection on what is or has been spoken or done. So often people acquire or engage in counsel from wrong voices, receiving and agreeing with conversation that is not from the Holy Spirit, but from the fleshly inclinations based on self motivation, personal issues, pain, jealousy, pride or rebellion. A person's mind must be open to be taught by the Holy Spirit on how to discern the voices and how to overcome them through the power of the WORD. I repeat again, thoughts can create dreams, visions *(true or false)* and pictures whether they are delusional or illusional. We cannot eat from everybody's table or tree or church.

Although the Bible warns us to test every spirit by the Spirit, the task is difficult when one doesn't recognize nor have their loins girded with the wisdom of Truth. Such things are toxic to the development of the GOD inheritance in, toward and upon you. In the garden, Satan offered a mixture; any mixture is toxic and vain. Such words, voices and situations are harmful to the character and identity of a believer. We must yearn for the voice of divine wisdom and act by the dominion given to us. The seed of Satan vibes are evil energy forces and we must be aware; such as resistant to Truth or indirect cunning methods to achieve something or win someone by wrong motivation. Many seek knowledge outside of the knowledge of GOD just has Eve done. It sounded good, yet it was the work of divination from the diseased seed of the wicked one. All that Satan presents leads to death. The first form of divination, the occult and witchcraft took place in the Garden of Eden. This reveals to us that confiding in the horoscope, crystal ball, communication with the dead, dream catcher, fortune-telling, fortune-cookies, water wishing and/ or stargazing are baits of darkness that many in the Church fall prey to. They are extremely seductive. I once was in bondage to the delusions and lies of water wishing, horoscopes, rabbit's foot, good luck charms and readings; unknowingly looking for answers or trusting in sources that were forbidden by the LORD. That is not our true identity. It's a marred image. The Spirit of GOD has broken many chains off of my mind and the LORD is no respect of persons. He shows no favoritism toward His children. The devil wants you to think and believe it is part of your inheritance. The LORD provision does not permit anything outside of Himself to promote direction, comfort, insight, answer to prayers or dictate one's character. Things of this nature's sway are to gain ones confidence and loyalty. The spirit behind these diabolic outlets is in pursuit of binding the soul. And when the soul leads denying the Light of the Holy Spirit it will hunger for such food. ***REPENT!*** *NO TRUTH OR LIGHT IS FOUND IN SATAN OR HIS WORKS.* Seeking to obtain knowledge, answers, a word, peace, direction, affirmation or destiny from such mediums is an abomination to the one true GOD and it is called idolatry. Total Chaos and Confusion! Truth is Light. The true Light corrects, exposes, breaks yokes and drives out darkness.

- *The Word of GOD declares in Exodus 20:4-5 Thou shall not make thee any graven image or any likeness of anything that is in heaven above or that is in the earth beneath or that is in the water under the earth. Thou shall not bow down thyself to them nor serve them: for I thy God am a jealous God, visiting the iniquity of the fathers upon the children unto the third and fourth generation that hate me...*

- **The Word of GOD declares in Genesis 1:14 And God said, Let there be light in the firmament of the heaven to divide the day from the night; and let them be for signs and seasons and days and years.**

ZODIAC

This is biblical truth not the occult!

Yahweh-Elohim created the heavenly bodies as signs to mark divine order and for the communication of His Holy calendar in human affairs; not for souls to seek or acquire knowledge or life predictions. Satan from the beginning has twisted and perverted the Truth. When Truth is perverted its substance and purpose is hidden. The lie and confusion are a joint rule of Satan's domain. When Truth is rejected or not revealed the ways of mankind will mirror a lie. This stage of delusion and illusion opens spiritual doors to pride, bondage, confusion, demonic visitations, alienation, fear, false identity, false perception, stubbornness and dullness of hearing or not recognizing the voice of GOD. Yahweh-Elohim, the Creator of the universe, created the stars, the moon, the sun, the planets and angels, but not for the purpose of personal prophecy. **The LORD is a jealousy GOD!** And He's jealousy over they that belong to Him *(the Body of Christ)*. Don't overlook His jealousy, it compares to no man's jealousy. Believers are restored as a new creation, renewed and regenerated in the divine **image of GOD** and commanded to worship the LORD GOD alone *{Exodus 20:3}*. Believers are forbidden to worship the Lord's creation or any manmade images. Yahweh's nature is the source of His libration to those that will put their trust in Him for everything and during troublesome times. The Body of Christ, just as the children of Israel, is commanded today to have no part in such adulterous activities. The new creation's direction, hope, insight, wisdom, future, characteristic traits and knowledge come from the SEED of Righteousness, the LORD; the maker of heaven and earth, the sea and all that is within them *{Psalms 146:6}*. The new creation, anyone in Christ, must seek, rely, depend and trust Him for all that concerns you. The new creation doesn't stand behind its birth zodiac. We, the Tribe of Judah, stand under the pavilion of the Blood Stain Banner of the Lion of Judah *(JESUS)* where there is no compromise or double standard. Yahweh still answers prayers, perform miracles and release blessings according to His set time.

The number twelve is found over 100 times in the Bible. Jacob had twelve sons and there were twelve tribes of Israel. Each of the twelve tribal leaders placed the assigned zodiac symbol on their tribal banners of color distinction *{Numbers 2}*. There are twelve foundations, twelve stones and twelve gates to the New Jerusalem *{Revelation 21:19-21}*. Also there were twelve disciples whom Yeshua named apostles *{Matthew 10:2}*. In **Isaiah 6:9** the prophet Isaiah prophesied the appointed time of the coming government of Yeshua HaMashiach. This prophecy did not come by his choice of doing or by self knowledge. It was communicated to the prophets from Yahweh. The prophet didn't go seeking celestial bodies or witches or warlocks for answers pertaining to life; they turned their face to GOD. This biblical insight informs us that the number twelve symbolize Yahweh's order, power, authority, foundation and government. It's All About Yahweh and His Creative Divine Order of unsealing a divine revelation or manifestation at the appointed time. As I researched the scripture, it reveals the twelve zodiac signs as prophetic time release symbols and divine principle *{Psalm 19:1-4}*.

Prophet Isaiah prophesied in **Isaiah 7:14** the virgin *(Mary)* will conceive and give birth to a son and call Him Immanuel; GOD with us. Virgo is the root of the word virgin which means unmarried or innocent. This scripture unlocks hidden revelation. Virgo in Hebrew is Bethulah (*virgin*); Greek is Parthenos (*the maid of virgin pureness*). As we step forward beyond the mythology of the Greeks to the Hebraic meaning which relates to the origin of a thing, one will discover the constellation mysteries behind the lies that unfolded by the Sumerian nation. The time GOD divinely revealed concerning the virgin birth pointed to the constellation sign Virgo which was revelation and the event on Yahweh's calendar in kairos *(due season or due measure)* to come to pass in chronos *(physical time)*. The constellations known as the zodiac virgo formed the image of the virgin maiden *(Mary)* holding a sheaf of wheat. Now from GOD to the Prophet Isaiah, GOD revealed His divine transaction, season and time of the Messiahs coming birth. Three symbols that wheat symbolizes are harvest, house of bread and life. The harvest season is another significant time on Yahweh's divine clock that relates to Israel and the Body of Christ. There are three Holy feasts in the harvest- fall season that are on Yahweh's divine clock *(Feast of Trumpets, Day of Atonement and Feast of Tabernacles)* and these three out of the seven are yet to be fulfilled at the appointed time. The Feasts of the LORD were appointed by Yahweh, not man and are thus prophetic. The revelation equips and prepares the Church to understand the season or time in which we live and what to expect. We may not fully comprehend all at once, but Holy Spirit will teach us Truth to cancel out the spirit of falsehood. When Yahweh assigned His Holy days and His feasts which symbolically points to Yeshua and reveals the mystery of the Holy days in regards to the Age of Grace and the Second Coming *(Greek: Parousia)* of Christ. He uses the sky

15

as a clock for calculating His time *{Genesis 1:14-19}*. The LORD orders the constellations to form alignment and moved by His Spoken WORD. Job asked a questioned in **JOB 38:32,** Can thou bring forth the sequence of the seasons or the constellations *(mazzaroth)* in their season or can you guide the bear with its children *(Ursa Major- the Big Dipper and Orion)*? These are zodiacs Job mentioned when he was on trial by his three friends during his crisis. Job informs us Yahweh has the last say about all things. No matter how we question GOD, His doings or find fault with GOD, with our self or others, He is the only one who can move and adjust time and situations to work for the believer's greater good and purpose of destiny. As a testimony, I was one that found fault with GOD and blamed GOD during a crisis. And just like Job I was bought to my knees and to a deep revelation of the awe of who GOD really is in the midst of a court case. **God's WORD rules the heavens and the universe.** And because things are done in His timing this teaches us to humble ourselves, learn and seek His face. Jesus said in the time of the end there will be a sign in the sky, the sign of the Son of man in heaven *{Matthew 24:30}*.

Another way to help you understand the true Biblical symbolism of the twelve zodiac signs is to imagine them as the hands on a clock and the sun *(greater light)* and moon *(lesser light)* as the numbers or fixed time of God's clock to manifest His events according to His divine calendar. The celestial bodies are the divided areas in the sky called stars that are different in spectrum, brightness and distance from the earth that respond to the Creator. They are in covenant relationship with Yahweh in governing the earth *{Genesis 1:16}*. All the celestial bodies know His language and He knows their language. Yeshua *(JESUS)* reveals Himself as the Alpha and the Omega, the beginning and the end, and the Bright and Morning Star *{Revelation 1:8, 17; 2:8; 22:13, 16}.* As a believer prays genuine heartfelt prayers and intercession they **supernaturally** bypass the moon, the planets and the sun and the constellation of the zodiac signs. When we walk by faith, seek the LORD by faith, ask by faith, decree by faith, live by faith, stand by faith, push by faith and pray **His WORD** by faith, then His WORD shifts the heavens on behalf of faith. He is faith, who dwells and tabernacles in the soul of believers. And when we pray faith within *(GOD)* connects with faith *(GOD)* that is far above all dimensional realms. GOD said, we are spiritual beings by DNA. *The Word of GOD declares in {James 5:16} The effectual fervent prayer of the righteous man avail much.* The believer's position in Christ elevates us above the other spheres and into the sphere that seats us with Christ in heavenly realms.

- *The Word of GOD declares in Ephesians 2:6 And hath raised us up together and made us sit together in heavenly places in Christ Jesus.*

- *The Word of GOD declares in Ephesians 2:13 But now in Christ Jesus you who once were far away have been bought near through the blood of Christ.*

- *The Word of GOD declares in Colossians 2:12 And having been buried with Him in baptism, you were raised with Him through your faith in the power of God, who raised Him from the dead.*

By choice people do as they please; yet, believers are to exercise in faith and perseverance the DNA universe within, the wind and fire of GOD that unites the believer to Him who causes the universe to align itself to give birth. **The Word of GOD declares in Romans 8:19 For creation waits eagerly for the sons of God to be revealed.** Why seek knowledge and purpose from creation when creation waits in expectation on the sons *(children led by the Holy Spirit)* of GOD to be revealed in the earth. We have been given direct access to the Heavenly Father in Christ through Ruach Hakodesh. This is what covenant lifestyle, true identity, sacrifice, trust, obedience and faith consist of. No matter how bad someone desires or attempts to justify their means of the zodiac or horoscope it is barred by the Law of Elohim. Yahweh has decreed that the totality of you "Be FREE!" The earlier astronomers and ancients understood God's time and purpose for the celestial bodies and the constellation of zodiac signs. The constellations were created to eliminate chaos by setting divine order and for Yahweh's visions *{Genesis 1:14}*. Mazzaroth *(mazzaloth)* is the Hebrew word for constellation also known as the zodiac. *[The zodiac is derived from the Greek meaning circle of animals. It is called the map of the sky. The Mesopotamians inherent their knowledge from the Sumerians. The Egyptians were credited for giving the constellations certain names linked to various weather patterns, people and demigods and goddess. This was the horoscope twisted perversion extended from the Babylonians (Mesopotamia 3200-500 BC), later introduced to the Greeks in the 4th century BC -Chaldean wisdom- for their personal belief and practices. This type of astrology in that age was referred to as the Hellenistic astrology (Wikipedia)].*

The horoscope is a chart used personally to obtain information about ones present or future and personalities and purpose from the heavens. Remember, Yahweh didn't use or permit it for that purpose. Now it sounds innocent, but it's a misguided and defiled resource.

Even if something came to pass the source in which it is spawned from is evil and corrupted. In the New Testament **Acts 16:16-18** the girl that earned a lot of money for predicting the future told true things about Apostle Paul. However, Apostle Paul discerned the spirit and commanded it to come out of her. She operated in divination totally opposite from operating in the gifts of the Holy Spirit. Throughout Bible history the Babylonians, Greeks, Egyptians and Romans practiced the abomination of idol worshiping. They practiced readings of the heavens by their works. These are they that rejected the Law of the Yahweh and despised the children of Israel. The pagans practiced astrology, necromancy and many other types of false religious rituals under the influence of their Greek gods and goddesses. The zodiac is not evil rather those who seek and idolize the zodiac. This type of astrology practice is rooted in **idolatry** *(anything that places created things in the position that only GOD should be in)* and forbidden by Yahweh *{2 King 17: 16-18; Deuteronomy 4:7; 18:18-22; Acts 3:22-23}.* The Day of the LORD will come like a thief; even the constellation, moon, sun and planets will be destroyed by fire and all that's done in the earth *{2 Peter 3:10}.*

- *The Word of GOD declares in Isaiah 47:13-14 All the counsel you have received has only worn you out. Let your astrologers come forward, those stargazers who make predictions month by month, let them save you from what is coming upon you. Surely they are like stubble; the fire will burn them up. They cannot even save themselves from the power of the flame. These are not coals for warmth; this is not a fire to sit by.*

- *The Word of GOD declares in Deuteronomy 18:9-13 When thou art come into the land which Jehovah thy God give thee, thou shall not learn to do after the abominations of those nations. There shall not be found with thee any one that make his son or his daughter to pass through the fire, one that use divination, one that practice augury, or an enchanter or a sorcerer or a charmer or a consulter with a familiar spirit or a wizard or a necromancer. For whosoever doeth these things is an abomination unto Jehovah: and because of these abominations Jehovah thy God doth drive them out from before thee. Thou shall be perfect with Jehovah thy God.*

The blood bought believer life is not governed by the movements of the heavenly bodies, the moon, sun, or planets. Covenant believers are governed by **God's Holy Word, Holy Spirit and His Authority and Power**. It is the Spirit of Christ that does the alterations within us, guides us, holds our future, predicts our future and is the influencer of our character and life. The new life in Christ is not the same pattern as the old life pattern without the Spirit and substance. Yeshua is the spiritual influencer who increases in the believer's relationship as we grow in the grace code. Pagan belief system has nothing in common with the one true GOD nor His sons and daughters. Any source outside of the will of GOD is off limits to the covenant believer. Close every door that the LORD has forbidden to be open and cut off all allegiances to the dark side and repent and rededicate your life back to the LORD. What does Baal have in common with Yahweh. *The Word of GOD declares in 1 Corinthians 10:20 No, I imply that what pagans sacrifice they offer to demons and not to God. I do not want you to be participants with demons.*

We are by birthright co-creators, as well as, co-labors with Christ. The sons of GOD possess a new mind that is not of this world. The new mind battles against the old thoughts and ways in the soul. The mind is the most valuable possession a soul has that is related to the spirit world. The counterfeiter, Satan, knows the strength of this great unlimited power. There was a saying that I use to hear my grandmother say decades ago, "That's bad seed or bad blood." In others words, you can't hang out with everyone or everywhere because your character, your mind may very well become tainted and corrupted, in thought first, then in behavior. *The Word of GOD declares in 1 Corinthians 15:33 Do not be mislead or fooled or deceived bad company corrupts good behavior, morals, or good character.* Remember, a spoken word or thought is seed and a seed purpose is to be productive. When a farmer plants he cast seed in order to produce a harvest. If the farmer does not cast his seed he will not get a return. What is planted creates the product of what is sown. When a bad seed is planted and take root, its method of bonding and corruption spreads in the soul. Satan, the author of confusion, is also the author of disorder, chaos, the master manipulator of twisting words and wants to fabricate his own family. The manipulator will manipulate the twisting of thought and words of people. As He communed with Eve she became confused, developed false impression and added to the command Elohim released for their safety. Remember, what is spiritual in the realm of the spirit world manifests itself in the realm of the physical world. The imagination of the thought dimension can take any soul into another dimension; negative or positive, heavenly or satanic. The creativity of thought is surfacing all around us daily from the Whitehouse to the school house, etc. Satan illegally stole and copied Yahweh's pattern and altered the good for his counterfeit unholy representation.

The two located atmospheres in the realm of the spirit with genetically electrical coding generates substance, presence, influence, character, behavior, promotion and demotion that are transported through spiritual portals *(unseen gates, doors)* into the physical realm and the human spirit. The realm of the Kingdom of Yahweh-Elohim DNA code is the realm of supernatural favor. It functions to illuminate, release favor, creativity, gifts and maturity. It also functions to counteract and purify all toxins from the bloodline *(lifeline)*, the spirit of fallen mankind due to the response to the devil's accusations and temptation in Eden. The **holy** or **unholy** seed -gene code- transmits through open portals into the soul through **active faith and obedience** or **active fear and rebellion** affecting the physical realm with good or evil under such persuasion. In the realm of the kingdom of darkness Satan's gene forms poisonous, diseased venom in the mind of the human spirit by infusing twisted truths, planting evil, spiteful motives, blinding the soul, corrupting the reasoning, afflicting, tormenting and darkening the soul or character of anyone. In the Kingdom of Light, the DNA provides the believer with abundant life, light and oil during all seasons and shields us from harm or injury, etc. The Spiritual DNA of the Spirit of Christ can symbolically be seen as a supernatural umbilical cord from heaven uniting the believer and providing the oxygen for substance, identity, sanctification, integrity, wholeness, union, fellowship, perfection in Christ and retribution in honor of those under His Governmental Kingdom Authority, Power and Love. **I AM THAT I AM** said, that He will not let anything take His chosen, the elect, by surprise; however, it is a promise with conditions. The Body of Christ must persistently and consistently remain in union. In addition: meditating, self examination, repentance and abiding in the Presence of Yahweh to hear and recognize what the Spirit is unveiling to the Body of Christ or what assault maybe intruding upon you for ambush concerning your birthright. The spiritual DNA of the Spirit of Truth will guide and reveal all Truth and show the believer things to come *{John 16:3}.* Ruach Hakodesh DNA overcomes the past, demolishes the illegal mind cycles and shows us how to be good stewards in the household of faith as strangers in this land.

The gene doesn't start from our immediate family generation, but it's the spiritual offspring of our fore-parents, ADAM *(Adam and Eve)*, in the Garden of Eden passing down the ancestry line. This is the resulting condition of the satanic spermicidal of the human heart, soul and mind of man with a plan to destroy the divine creative order of Yahweh in the land. The fall contaminated the totality of man's trichotomous *(spirit, soul and body- illustration B- chapter 4)*. That which was turned upside down by the fall is now made right side up by grace and faith DNA. The chaotic order darkened the spirit which made it absence of Light. This order means the **soul** would rule the **body** by outward influences through the gates of the senses; **dichotomous**. The SEED of Christ places divine order for the new birth; meaning the Spirit *(GOD)* that quickens rules the soul and the body. The created divine order, when GOD breath and man became a living soul, is **Spirit, soul and body** *(illustration C- chapter4).* The act of open defiance and rebellion opened a spiritual portal which brought in generational curses, sin, offenses, incest, decay, development of false religions, alienation, hostility toward the One true GOD, sickness, disease, turmoil, witchcraft, familiar spirits, divination, human sacrifice, idol worship, worldly appetite, bondage, defeat, hardship, division, loss of vision, hatred, murder, slander, harassment, loss of submission, loss of authority, loss of dominion, ownership, position, loss of fellowship, loss of sonship communion and finally the loss of true identity. That which was unconscious became awaken by an unrestrained evil desire that gave the right of way and ushered in enslavement under the authority and power of Satan, the god of this world.

SOUL TIES

The birthright *(identity inheritance)* of humanity was stolen and replaced by all types of falsehood that came by the deceptive sound that won the trust, the ear and the eye gate of mother Eve. Those imagines which appeared to look right, feel right and be right even though they were false gained access. This contributed to the first ungodly spiritual soul-tie and the law of being spiritually unequally yoked together. A yoke formed through the attraction of wickedness will always lead souls from the Truth of GOD and off of the straight and narrow path of righteousness. Everything is not what it appears to be. Note: The appearance of evil doesn't always appear to have the look that it is evil; there's a tendency of finding out after being hooked. Nevertheless, there is a hidden agenda by the unseen evil force that is at work. Someone or something can be well put together, taste good, feel good or sent to suit your quality of physical needs at the right time, yet it's deadly to your system in the long run. Situations are easy to get into, but hellish to break from. Christians are cautioned to abstain from all appearances of evil *{1 Thessalonians 5:22}*. **Ungodly** soul-ties are deadly to anybody's **spiritual freedom**. Soul-ties are good if they are a **godly** yoke which bind with like spirits. A soul-tie, godly or ungodly, is the activity of a spirit that carries the weight like a heavy chain link in the realm of the soul that knits or enslaves the soul to respond to its call. This is why it is called a soul-tie. Its power actually blinds and ties souls together. Soul-ties are tridimensional meanly they can have delayed affects on your mind, emotions, feelings, body and actions. Ungodly soul-ties can exist from one relationship to the next and the next with a leading trail until it is broken and restoration begins. When GOD saves and deliver us, we should not have a continual taste for the worldly appetite knowing that appetite will lead us out of the will of GOD. Females by the God-given nature are nurturers, givers, conquerors and more; males by the God-given nature are providers, pursuers, visionaries, protectors and more *{Genesis 2:15,18}*. Women may be more emotional and open hearted; while men may be observers, thinkers in thought instead of allowing the feelings to lead. Remember, Eve was in another location that dealt with her affections and Adam was perhaps in another frame of thought. Some of us tend to be more trusting; while others may be private, curious, withholding or defensive. If someone has been deeply hurt, use or abused in some kind of way or sexually active outside of their marriage or involved in promiscuous sexual practices ungodly soul-ties can form from such activity and cause that soul to yearn for its attraction long after it's over. Spiritually, demons can transfer and will until the right of way is no longer available. This open door leads to other things. For example: when one meets someone else the emotions and mind reacts as if they are still connected to the past relationship. The mind causes the body to react to emotions as if part of it is incomplete or not satisfied; making it difficult to move forward by gripping or building a fortified place in the mind. When sexual acts, whether penetrated or others sexual pleasures are performed outside of the marriage covenant it is first of all in the eyes of GOD ungodly and not sanctioned or honored. It deals with the inner parts of the person(s) involved. And some sexual practices aren't GOD ordained. GOD created sex which is healthy, good and pleasurable to be between a man and woman in legal covenant grace. The sexually intimacy itself creates a covenant. When people sleep around ungodly covenants are forming bonds naturally, as well as, mentally and emotionally. The giving of oneself is not only physical, but spiritual. GOD created sex and sex is what is meant by bone of my bone and flesh of my flesh; the two shall now be one *(spirit, mind and body);* the consummation of the two. As a result of ungodly soul ties being formed and relations have been broken and persons have moved on, most likely one or both emotional states have not moved on. Now apart of the last person is with them mentally. This can show itself through action and response. Even though sex is a physical act it carries with it what I call a spiritual tag to the soul and heart. For some people sex is just sex; while for others it involves inner attachment, a sense of belonging, gratification, commitment and deep affection. Spiritual transmitted demons can freely travel unnoticed into the next relationship with its hidden agenda that will manifest in the soul; even the act of adultery has its share of spiritual tags. This can open doors to vulnerability, comparison, loss of self control, anger, low self-esteem, fatal attraction, stalking, insensitivity, over sensitivity and etc. If ungodly soul-ties aren't destroyed they will prevent a meaningful relationship from existing and can slowly devalue a person from within. When spirit knits itself it becomes one spiritually. Those spirit tags must be renounced, rejected openly, severed and casted out by the power of GOD, through a conscious mind, an act of faith, determination and submission. A soul must desire to be free from anything or anyone or any group that is forbidden by GOD. The appetite has to change! And that starts by breaking ungodly covenants.

Eve knew the tree of knowledge of good and evil was not good for purpose; however, she consistently continued to entertain its seductive appeal not realizing over a period of time that there was an entity behind the scene linking and tying their soul to his spirit and they desired more. Adam's outlook, thoughts, mind and heart became flawed in Eden through the serpent's whisper. However, because Yahweh is holy, longsuffering and just His Supernatural Provision Code of Redemption was inaugurated before the foundation of the world to re-establish identity through the His DNA that would wipe out every curse, destroy ungodly soul-ties, wickedness, create a clean heart and renew a right spirit through submission. The incorruptible SEED overthrew the gates of hell and opened the heavenly portal for all who would trust Him in order to receive the birthright inheritance through the DNA of Yeshua HaMashiach *(Jesus the Christ)*. The promises and blessings that had been lost are now available through the **Cross**. The righteous wealthy Holy One of Israel in the form of SEED exited the realm of Glory to be born in the physical realm to destroy the curse, the lie, the cycle and the seed of Satan. For that moment Yeshua HaMashiach laid aside **His Glory, His Majesty, His Riches and His Royalty** to become poor; clothed in human flesh in the likeness of man; yet the incarnated, GOD and man.

Deliverance Prayer:

In the Name of Jesus Christ by the Authority and Power of the Holy Spirit I Renounced _____, _____, _____ and Command Every Ungodly Soul-Tie to Break Off Of Me In the Name of JESUS CHRIST. In the Name of JESUS CHRIST By the Authority of the Holy Spirit I Command Every Death Cycle or Ungodly Mind Patterns To Be Canceled In the NAME OF JESUS CHRIST. In the Name of Yeshua HaMashiach (Jesus Christ) I Command Every Unclean Spirit to Lose Me And Those Doors to be Closed Forever In the Powerful, Matchless Name of Jesus, _____. Lose Me In the Name of JESUS CHRIST. BREAK IN THE NAME OF JESUS! I Command Every Unclean Spirit of Resistant and Torment To Be Gone From Me, Out of Me, In the Name of JESUS CHRIST. I Command Every Residue of My Pass to Dry Up In the Name of JESUS CHRIST. In the Name of JESUS CHRIST I Command Every Voice of the Pass To Be Silent In My New Life, New Heart, New Walk and New Mind From This Moment Forward. I Command My Mind, My Thought, My Heart, My Tongue and My Actions To Be In Alignment With The Mind of CHRIST...Blood Washed and Purge Me Holy Spirit IN JESUS NAME.

Illustration A - Open Heaven Atmosphere - Shaded areas represents the Image and Glory Presence

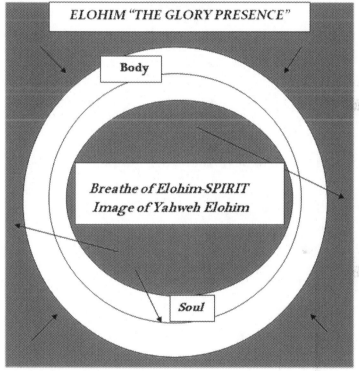

Cause me to hear Your loving kindness in the morning, for in You do I trust; cause me to know the way in which I should walk, for I lift up my soul to You.

Psalm 143:8

2

GENETICS AND GENESIS

In 1997 my husband and I experienced a crisis during my pregnancy with our first born who is deceased. That experience later opened a peculiar door for me to begin my personal research and study on genetics, genes, chromosomes and DNA. During and after my pregnancy I hoped that our baby boy's genetic abnormality could've been surgically corrected by the genetic doctors. However, the deletion of half of one of the forty-six chromosomes which carries protein cells for a complete gene makeup is not something doctors have the capability to restore. The chromosome's aberration of the deleted portion of chromosomal DNA makes up a significant difference in the ability for someone to function, such as, personality, behavior, features, physical condition, deformity, neurological, psychological and physiological as a complete being. The genes which are housed inside the chromosome *(an incomplete pair in our case)* was due from the nonstructural abnormality in the deletion of what is called the p-arm; a half of a single chromosome. This is associated with a biochemical link for creating the internal and external chemical process for proper cell function, proteins and genes; which correlates with the brain and nervous system. The physical makeup composition was thrown out of alignment. Study shows the human genetic make up consists of a set of 23 chromosome pairs; one set from the father and one set from the mother for the complete identity of an individual's total makeup. The mutation of the genetic gene can affect the whole being in many different ways internal, as well as, external. Remember, the brain and nervous system are major components in these circumstances; yet in the fall in Eden there was also a biochemical shift in the bio of mankind. The internal will and spirit that was affected resulted in external characteristics developing gradually into flaws. This is the genetic encoding of ADAM *(mankind)* after the fall. It became entwined with the human bloodline. That one act of disobedience sent a stream of poison into the souls of mankind; soul, mind and body.

As I began this study, Holy Spirit unveiled the understanding and revelation of how the natural human gene functions are closely related to the spiritual DNA in the soul of mankind in the regenerated state and in the degenerated state. When something is coded, it has been wired or charged to act, function and respond by an inborn nature that way by its manufacturer. That inherent code produces the characteristics of that thought, will and desires in the behavior. Therefore, a recoding by a negatively charged energy cell would erase or reverse the entire wiring of the mind slowly by indoctrination by another reflection producing a counterfeit image or doctrine of belief causing the soul to look the same outwardly temporarily; however, functioning improperly in character.

The counterfeit reprogramming can teach its offspring how to camouflage and how to do as he does, when entangled with the mind and spirit. This goes on a lot in the church; yet GOD is able to see the inner heart and its motives. GOD wants us sound, sober and alert at all times; sharp in the Spirit. It's the power of His DNA. As a believer is being sharpened in the Spirit, we will shift locations when temptation knocks at the door; be focused, quick to pray, quick to listen and slow to speak, but ready with a seasoned word of faith. This is a life time walk nothing magical.

There are many diseases and disorders that can pass down genetically through the bloodline of mankind; DNA encodings that have spiritually passed through the spiritual womb or through generations. They pass through lack of knowledge, rebellion, brainwashing, cloning or counterfeit, after its kind that duplicates the reproducing of another representation. Satan's DNA is perverse and unholy in nature. Elohim's DNA is righteous and holy in nature. Remember, the DNA is what makes up the total you. Adam's DNA is who he is; his identity did not come from the cosmos or the earth or sky. Mankind's identity has always originated from the thought of Yahweh and His Ruach *(Spirit)*. We may look outwardly like our parents or other relatives outwardly and even possess similar distinguishing qualities. We may also have characteristics that reach several generations back; however, the inner most being has an identity of its own designed by the Creator's SEED of coding. Therefore, because the code of design is wind *(Spirit)*, it longs to connect with the spiritual in some form. The spirit seeks to trace and link with its Creator through blueprint memory. Our renewed spirit, not flesh, has a spiritual blueprint of remembrance. Yet, our flesh, the eternal sensory system and the worldly system can throw barricades that cause the human senses, vision and psyche *(mind)* to become spiritually blurred and spiritually blind. In the cosmic *(spirit world)* the wrong frequency channels can open wrong doors and release wrong spirits. On the other hand, faith-filled spoken words followed by obedience can open up the portals of heaven and release manifested promises. For this reason, as believing believers we must center our mind, our hearts and souls on heavenly things and not on things of this world system. The Ekklesia's *(church)* new nature must be fed the Truth continuously; they must be seekers of the one true living GOD. Ruach Hakodesh *(Holy Spirit)* will breathe divine mass upon the faith seed for Himself to expand within your hearts and minds swelling to flow over from you into others or simply being a light in dark places.

The psyche *(mind)* is where creativity, thought, motivation and actions are reflected first directing the body's reactions. The mind is very courageously powerful; yet, it can be dangerous under the wrong influence, but effective under the right influence. The devil's plan of execution is to kill the coding of the DNA GOD-gene by destroying the original blueprint image of the Spirit. The blueprint was created in the image of Elohim. And the devil's plan was to steal the position of estate and erase the Creator's thought-handprint and replace it with false perception, false information, false revelation, false hope and lies. Thus, creating an unholy wicked blueprint. These transactions darken the spirit of a man and placed the soul in a false reality that was never favored by Yahweh-Elohim. The soul became delusional and placed in a state of spiritual hostility towards the Creator and His way. Whether one believes it or not reality is that there is an unseen diabolic atmosphere with evil spirits working behind the visible realm in which we inhabit. Apostle Paul warns the Church, not the world, of such things which were revealed by Christ to him and how to combat the odds. We witnessed how the devil used the serpent to brainwash Eve. Today the adversary will use whatever and whoever to remove our minds and hearts far from Truth. This atmospheric sphere is not discerned by the physical body or the natural eye *{1 Corinthians 2:14}* it can only be discerned in the Holy Spirit. This can be easily compared to how angels work on behalf of believers although they are not seen with the natural eye.

We can see the evidence that words are very powerful and effective even when a soul doesn't understand the worth of their legal birthright. The mind will fall prey to the enemy's bait due to weakness. This type of weakness comes from not being knowledgeable and not relying on the Word of GOD. The enemy spoke his thought openly to Eve through the serpent in a cunning way which was very swaying and appealing to her senses. The words formed a lie *(painted a picture)* and entertained her imagination. After indulging intimately with the shrewd reasoning of the devil, his seed -DNA- penetrated her senses, mind and soul. Sin was conceived and sin gave birth to transgression and iniquity. Now the lie that was perceived as truth manifested in the physical realm through a legal door. As this door opens lustful craving and desires of lust manifested. Eve, mother of all humanity, experienced the power of wickedness and then signed a spiritual covenant agreement with Satan thus, turning from Yahweh. Eve ate then Adam willingly believed the lie that produced Satan's evil genetic offspring. Adam and Eve were now intimately **one** spirit, **one** mind, **one** soul and **one** body with the counterfeiter. As they willfully agreed with each other and the adversary, they turned their eyes, hearts, wills and backs to Yahweh, their first love. Now sin entered with its blindness depositing spiritual and physical death. We don't have to succumb to the inclinations of the flesh feelings. When your flesh is in a weak vulnerable state, you must exercise your faith to step out of that place of darkness. Whenever your flesh gets the best of you and it seems as if you are stuck or in a rut, remember, God's provision has made ransom for all.

- ***The Word of GOD declares in Romans 8:5-9 For they that are after the flesh do mind the things of the flesh; but they that are after the Spirit the things of the Spirit. For to be carnally minded is death; but to be spiritually minded is life and peace. Because the carnal mind is enmity against God: for it is not subject to the law of God, neither indeed can be. So then they that are in the flesh cannot please God. But ye are not in the flesh, but in the Spirit, if so be that the Spirit of God dwell in you.***

We perish because of the lack of knowledge which brings about disobedience and doubt; first in thought then action. Divine knowledge goes beyond the human intellectual capacity of understanding, thinking and reasoning. It powerfully overrides the enemies of our soul that we come in contact with face to face in this walk of life. This Wisdom or Knowledge which comes from the DNA of Ruach Hakodesh will change any present situation, revert attacks or lies from the enemy, your outlook, disposition and reasoning. I am a living testimony of the importance of having the virtue of an ear to hear what the Spirit of the LORD is saying. And after hearing, **HEED! Follow! Obey** the instructions of GOD in the face of opposition that comes to disgrace and assassinate your character in Christ, strip your identity and with a devised plan to lead you on a wrong path. It only takes a moment. Free will is a priceless gift that allows us to make our own choices. However, because free will is a constitution it should be governed and sanctified by the Word of GOD and placed under the guidance of the Fire of GOD. Again wrong paths, wrong directions from wrong choices leads to identity theft through Satan's vices and tactics. That's his game and his playground turf, but you are not to be deceived. **"I Decree That You Operate in the Power of Holy Ghost and Not your own strength."** Make your confession, "I will LORD." Sometimes we may cry or lash out because it hurts making the flesh carnal nature bow down to Truth. In fact, the carnal mind never wants to be wrong, but the WORD of GOD will show the mind of the flesh up every time and that's His DNA in action to bring correction and maturity. Jesus proclaimed a very personal truth regarding His branches' welfare and atmosphere. He prophesies to us today that outside of Him we cannot do anything *{John 15:5}*. The essence of the fruit is developed in you as He grows in you. The branches must stay connected to the True Vine, which is the source of divine life for everyday living. Remaining in Christ forces the Hand of GOD by His Spirit to supply your every need. Obedience is manifested love that comes out of a soul that loves GOD. When obedience is at the heart of the temple, that temple is filled with the dwelling of the Lord *{John 14:23}*. That's a promise with attached blessings under an open heaven.

Demonic spirits have faces that can manifest through any soul that has given a door for evil thoughts to breathe, fester and grow. Remember, the seed is planted for penetration; afterwards seedlings begin to sprout for growth. Unclean spirits also called evil spirits and evil minds will reveal themselves through rage, greed, jealousy, bitterness and even impurity exposing itself through souls that have lent their facilities to darkness in turn giving the unclean spirit a body to act through. We witnessed this with Adam and Eve. No matter what speaks in volume by sight the Eternal Word of GOD takes dominion over the pride of life, the lust of the eyes and the lust of the flesh in the realm of the soul. As long as your heart is unadulterated the Blood of YESHUA and your angels are standing at attention ready to be released at the sound of the WORD. Ready to perform His Word concerning all that concerns you. And that's real talk! No devil! No demon in hell can defeat or stand equal with **the Blood, the Word, and the Name of Jesus or the Authorize Power**

of Yahweh in Christ JESUS, the Ruach. Yes, one word of divine knowledge spurned in the spiritual womb will birth divine substance to deliver any soul out of a distressed situation. We have to push and give birth. It's spiritual work, like a pregnant woman giving birth. It will also deliver one from a spiritual poverty mentality into true spiritual prosperity and divine creativity of purpose.

Prayer

By the Power of GOD in the Name of JESUS, I Plead the Blood of JESUS Over My Destiny, Over My Senses, Desires and Affections. I Decree That My senses, Desires, Affections and Sensitivity Become Supernaturally Awakened Through the Power of the Holy Spirit to the Will of GOD in the Name of JESUS. I Will Live and Not Die!

Amen.

Now all that is of great wealth, in some spiritual cases, will be reduced to abnormality through the wooing and desensitizing by the vices of worldliness and weights on the carnal mind. This action of becoming less sensitive to the voice of the Holy Spirit will be accepted as being normal which results from the blinding of hearts and minds through deception. Desensitization is the act of getting farther from the Light of consciousness and the voice of Truth that the Spirit's voice may begin to sound foreign or diluted resulting in absence of hearing. This happens even today in the Church. When someone is incarcerated in the mind or in a dead zone for a length of time, the ruling nature will adapt to it conditions not realizing the sleep- grave danger. Look at the spiritual state of the nation as a whole today. Many are blindly accepting pathways, the ways of the world, policies and laws that defy the very nature, identity and structure of Yahweh GOD and His creative order in the earth realm. For example: dishonoring the sanctuary of the LORD by allowing unsanctioned activities or programs to occur for fleshly entertainment and hype. In addition, the passing of laws that oppose the laws GOD established for the land, such as, same sex marriages, open marriages, transgender restroom rights, firearms freedom and prayer banned from schools. When something that isn't right, yet lives, behaves or looks a certain way for a period of time often becomes normal and tolerable to some mindsets. All abominable offspring draw from the demonic gene and is an abomination in the eyes of Yahweh. The LORD GOD does not change and neither should the Ekklesia *(the Church)*, which is the Body of Christ and is filled with Holy Spirit! Walking in the fruit of love unction's the Christian to stand up for righteousness sake, bless those that curse us and pray for those that despitefully use us. God's plan comes loaded with divine protection and divine promises for the faithful and obedient. We're always in GOD thoughts. *The Word of GOD declares in Jeremiah 29:11 For I KNOW the THOUGHTS I Think toward you, saith the LORD, thoughts of peace, and not evil, to give you an expected end.* Glory! He's releasing the revelation of that created work for the faithful even now!

As Adam walked with Elohim in the cool of the day he was submerged in the treasury of wealth called the GLORY, the Presence of Yahweh. Adam's manifested thoughts were powerful expressions translated from the Glory Spectrum of Light. Therefore, Adam walked and created in all dominion in the bands of Divine Glory. As Elohim spoke or thought, Adam visibly created the reality of that image or thought that was woven into his fabric. He was mobilized in the glorious Presence because that was his DNA environment -his identity- his atmosphere- who he was and who he worshiped and belonged to! There is no separation or two in the spectrum of one; **the unity of power is one**. Adam knew all things in the glorious Presence! Adam experienced the pure, genuine fellowship with the Creator until Eve's free will appetite was aroused which resulted in Adam's free will and weakness toward the persuasive sway of his wife. And that appetite led to the first apostasy.

Greek term for Apostasy
Apostasia: backsliding, disownment, rejection,
defection from truth (action of falling away)

Adam's frequency of communication with GOD existed only through divine counsel and the wisdom of Yahweh infused through him for Glory fulfillment. The language was **one** and the mind was **one**. Adam knew the voice of GOD. He knew the presence of the LORD. Adam was no stranger to the Shekinah Glory of GOD. It is the supernatural cosmic within itself in ADAM. Adam's covenant was **spiritual** not religious or carnal. It was the way of covenant life and it maximized the divine capacity through continual obedience, commitment, agreement and intimacy in the Glory of Yahweh *(the* LORD*)*. If you ever want to know what's on the heart of GOD about you, I beseech you to get in His Presence. Adam was wired, structured and coded to function in an open heaven. "It was his habitation." Every kingdom has to survive in its own habitation; outside of its habitation is adaptation or death. For example: fish cannot survive outside of water. A wolf cannot survive in your home, but could possibly be tamed to adapt under extreme conditions. When a believer backslides he learns to adapt to conditions that are not favorable to his true character or his inner man. And when a Christian becomes lukewarm or cold we are outside of our habitation. When we become one with the weights of worry, pride, frustration, lack of self control, lust, greed, faithlessness or isolation we are outside of our habitation. Therefore, we must break any cord of such agreement. ***The Word of GOD declares in Amos 3:3 Can two walk together, except they agree.*** The work of agreement that manifests comes out of the spirit -mind- that is in agreement. The **union of covenant** foundation has always been spiritual, as well as, natural.

Hebrew & Greek terms for Covenant
Berith: constitution, agreement, alliance between God and man
Diatheke: legal binding declaration with benefits

Greek term for Cosmos
Kosmos: ordered system, worldly affairs, creation, the world

Adam *(Eve)* was uniquely and supernaturally infused genetically with creative divine order, intensified greatness, holiness, perfection, immortality, radiance and weight with full of supremacy in EDEN. The GLORY of GOD filled the atmospheric paradise in EDEN. As Adam who was king spoke out of the mind of the Elohim through the abiding Presence of the Glory he shows us the royalty of dominion-ship the church is inborn with and what happens when we are under the Glory cloud. Remember, JESUS walked on water, cast out demonic spirits and healed the woman who had leprosy and commanded peace to overcome nature, being filled with the fullness of the Shekinah Glory. Yeshua defied the laws of time, gravity and space and functioned by the Laws of Creative *(Divine)* Order. We as "the Church" have not seen, heard nor experienced who we really are or what we are in Christ. Nor do we really have the full understanding as a whole what we really possess in Christ. It's not enough just to go to a church when the Bible tells us we are the church. The image of Elohim is more than just an image. The DNA contains the image and the Glory substance and the system that contains our nature and characteristics. Because of the image and the Presence of the Glory of Yahweh-Elohim, the souls in Christ are entitled to function in dominion, authority, creativity, productivity and vision as Elohim created us to do. How do we do this? By Faith and spirit-filled sober teaching. Elohim desires for the household of faith to rise to this level of divine revelation and to abide supernaturally in the blueprint of our habitation. This habitation causes open heaven reality experiences. The universe is birthed from Elohim. The universe was formed by Him first in specific order with details for Him. All that Elohim created was for Him. Satan, full of pride, was filled with iniquity sinning from the beginning. Lucifer wearing the crown of pride desired the crown of dominion-authority, crown of wisdom and glory that was once experienced by him before he sinned in heaven. Now the Crown of Authority was given legally to ADAM. All that Elohim had was divinely and genetically imparted to Adam completely. Adam had the world and the universe in his hand. Selah! That means the King's business was under ADAM's dominion and rule. EVERYTHING! Elohim who created the universe entrusted *elohim* to fill it as He would. Deep is calling unto deep. The SEED DNA GOD-gene genetically generated the course of divine destiny for *elohim*-ADAM. The key instruction was to consciously fellowship with the Tree of Life that beamed the wisdom of remaining in covenant agreement, a covenant branded in devoted affectionate loving communion with Yahweh-Elohim *(Godhead)* through the act of willful obedience, love and trust. This revelation reveals the significant value of recognizing, understanding, adhering and walking in your GOD-gene identity in Christ.

Elohim (Strong One) is found 2602 times in the Old Testament. The title is used interchangeability for the True God Elohim denoting His majesty, honor, fullness and actions. It also denotes the authority and the power over powers: used for false gods, supernatural spirits (angels), and human leaders (Kings, Judges and Messiah). Elohim plural for El, descriptive title used for Yahweh, He is the GOD of gods meaning Elohim of elohim- lower than GOD {Deuteronomy 10:17; Psalms 136:2}. However, mere men are not to be worshipped as GOD, not to be placed a pedestal, but are authorize and commissioned representatives to carry out the laws of Yahweh in the earth through Christ in faith and obedience and love. Yeshua, the last ADAM, restored the dominion that the first Adam lost through his blood back to each believing faithful Church.

Deuteronomy 10:17

For the LORD your God is God of gods, and Lord
of lords, a great GOD, a mighty, and a terrible,
which regard not persons, take reward:

Psalms 8:5

You made him a little less than divine, but you crowned
him (believers) with glory and honor (in Christ).

Psalms 82:6

I said, ye are gods; you are all sons of the Most High

Psalms 136:2

O give thanks unto the GOD of gods; for his mercy endures forever.

John 10:34

Jesus said, is it not written in your law, I said ye are gods (elohim).

The Ruach of the Living GOD desires to make His dwelling in
the sanctuary called the believer. The human body is symbolically
described as a temple or sanctuary for the filling and dwelling of the
Spirit of the Living GOD. From the Genesis to revelation it is shown
to us that GOD has always desired to tabernacle *(dwell-fellowship)*
with His chosen people. We should desire the settling Presence of the
LORD to connect with the indwelling of His Presence within us at
those appointed times. Sin removes the Glory Presence and obedience

brings the Glory Presence of GOD; this happens and causes change. Change prophetically represents the unpopular and unknown; and attracts friction. Change is not popular, but it a Law of the Kingdom of GOD. Everything that came into contact with Yeshua was changed; nothing remained the same that was out of alignment in the Presence of GOD. The time is upon the Church *(believer)* to become intolerant of the itchy-ear syndrome preaching that makes the flesh feel good; yet, no power to destroy the yokes that bind souls while the spirit suffers to indulge in the Presence of GOD. The fleshly syndrome produces no inner heartfelt or mind stimulated transformation. GOD desires that His body experiences His Glory invasion. ***The Word of GOD declares in 2 Corinthians 3:17 Now the Lord is that Spirit: and where the Spirit of the Lord is, there is liberty.*** We need and must invite the Presence of the Lord to reside in us so we can experience true change. When the Ruach of Christ invades by invitation into the worship of the CHURCH there will be a mass revival like never before. The hunger and the thirst for a divine interception that is received into the nostrils of the Most High will stir Him to hear from heaven, heal the mind, the heart and the soul of those that hunger and thirst for righteousness and stir Him to come settle in the midst of His worshipers. It is God's will to break chains, destroy yokes of bondage, deep hurt, rejection, loneliness, idleness, overthrow the throne of false doctrine. Yeshua Is Already Ready To Be Unleashed to establish in the hearts of those who will believe, already believe and are ready to step outside of self into the next faith dimension.

- ***The Word of GOD declares in 1 Peter 4:17 For the time is come that judgment must begin at the house of God: and if it first begin at us, what shall the end be of them that obey not the gospel of God?***

Yeshua is the Same Yesterday, Today and Forevermore! He Changes Not! Grace and Truth is the complete antidote provided by ABBA to supernaturally transfer the divine nature code. Christ Jesus my Mediator, High Priest, Redeemer, Advocate and Judge has the Authority and the Power to overthrow every defiled blood issue in the spirit, the mind, the heart and the soul that you may be wrestling or challenged with today. He makes the heart and mind fit not only to come into His Presence, but to abide under the shadow of His Presence triumphing over the enemies of the soul and the Holy Spirit filling the temple.

It is a powerful strength, assurance, position, place of safety and weapon of force to know who and whose you are concerning your spiritual birthright as a citizen of the Kingdom of GOD. You are chosen by Yeshua HaMashiach *(Jesus the Christ)*. The renewed mind is to be an established pattern of the mind of Christ. The community of faith will encounter assaults and temptations. And some will be indirectly while others are directly. They come whether we are expecting them or not. When you are truly walking with GOD, the devil will throw fiery darts and manifest his evil presence through anyone whose mind-heart is open and available with intent to remove the crown from the head of the king or queen. The Church *(Ekklesia)* is the target of the devil mainly because it is the spiritual institution in the earth that has been given the highest position with Christ to partake in delegating the bidding of ABBA in the earth realm through the Authority and Power of Holy Spirit. The DNA of the Ekklesia wreaks havoc on every evil force because Christ is the head of the body. The devil as he performed in EDEN will seek to roar or work through any to attempt to shut down your walk-life of faith, the anointing, remove the crown, take the kingly-priestly authority, shut down your consistency, your progress, your devotion, shut down your covenant-bond with GOD, seek to move you out of position, off focus, off guard and off watch. He wants to steal from each believer what he once possessed; a heavenly, priestly, kingly position in the Royal Kingdom Court of Yahweh-Elohim under the Glory. Satan attempts to demoralize, break, destroy and divert believers into the carnal sinful nature in order to keep the believer from going forward obtaining every redemptive spiritual blessing in Yeshua HaMashiach. *The Word of GOD declares in 1 John 4:1 believers not to believe every spirit, but test the spirits by the Spirit to discern if the spirit is from GOD.* We must be full of the Word and full of the Spirit in this season and not full of the world, worldliness or self in order to spiritually discern the difference. These two territories are contrary to each other just as: grace DNA and corruption DNA will never be reconciled, neither can Satan and a sanctified soul.

Prayer

Heavenly Father, I Give Thanks to You for My Heavenly Inheritance. In the Name of JESUS by the Authority and the Power of the Ruach Hakodesh, I Command Every Ungodly Soul-tie to be Broken Off of My Soul and Bloodline! I Decree the Power of the Blood of JESUS and the Sword of the Spirit Sever the Umbilical Cord of ALL That is Contrary to the Will of GOD In the Name of JESUS. I Command the Infrared Darts of the enemy to be Terminated By the Power of the Consuming Fire of Holy Spirit In the Name of JESUS!

Amen.

Because the Power of GOD frees us, we war in the Spirit and by the Spirit to maintain and walk in our deliverance. There is a conflict between Truth and falsehood, flesh and Spirit, wickedness and righteousness, holy and unholy, clean and unclean, genuine and counterfeit, good and evil. Yeshua came not to bring the peace that many thought He would bring, but Yeshua brought a divine peace, a Spiritual Sword that decapitates spiritual so called giants which opposes divine order. The governing authority and the influential power of persuasion by the Ruach Hakodesh *(Holy Spirit)* has dominion over and against sin's diabolic powers of unclean spirits that set up fortresses in the minds and hearts of many souls. Just because one is saved and has received Jesus Christ, does not excuse anyone. It doesn't stop, block, exempt or lock out the fiery darts of the enemy's evil influences, schemes and assassination darts or flesh inclinations from targeting the new creature. The accuser deliberately sends target signals like that of infra-red. He sends fiery darts for penetrating destruction of your faith and for destruction of the DNA -righteous seed. The Ekklesia has nothing to fear. Hold your faith up like that of an armored shield that protects against attacks thrown toward your righteousness in Christ. The Bride of Christ has been given the highest privilege, crowned with dominion, glory, authority and power to dismantle every evil policy of the accuser of the brethren. We apprehend it by taking a righteous stance in the strategy code of grace reflected in the heart, mind, soul and body of a genuine believer by the Glory of ABBA. The power rests upon His SEED and the SEED mobilize the believer in the Spirit. Activating the knowledge of who you are in Christ will back up the enemy. No longer will you be thrown off course into limbo by the threats or tricks of the adversary because the LORD has made Himself your refuge and shelter in times of trouble.

- *The Word of GOD declares in Genesis 3:15 And I will put enmity between you (Satan) and the woman, between your offspring (seed-children) and her seed (Christ-the church); He (Christ) will crush your head (Satan) and you will strike his heel.*

Christ's human sufferings and death for the world in its entirety points to Satan bruising his heel *{Genesis 3:15}*; therefore, through death and the resurrection a fatal charge sent execution to the sphere of darkness and its ruler. *The Word of GOD declares in Isaiah 53:5-7 He was wounded for our transgressions, he was bruised for our iniquities; and the chastisement of our peace was upon HIM; with His stripes we are healed.* Yeshua HaMashiach got up with All the Keys! All Victory, All Rank, All Dominion, All Honor, All Glory and All Power! Yeshua is KING! Yeshua has All Authority! He Reigns with Power and an Iron Scepter; demolishing sin, strongholds, curses, perversions and wickedness. *The Word of GOD declares in Colossians 2:15 Having disarmed the rulers and authorities of their power, Yeshua-Jesus made a public spectacle of them, triumphing over them by the cross.* The Cross of Christ established complete victory over death and sin.

- *The Word of GOD declares in Colossians 2:10 {NIV} So you are complete through your union with Christ, who is the head over every ruler and authority.*

- *The Word of GOD declares in Ephesians 1:19-22 {ESV} and the unlimited greatness of His power for us who believer, according to the working of His mighty strength which He brought about in Messiah-Christ when he raised Him from the dead and seated Him at His right hand in the heavenly realm. Yeshua is far above every rule and authority and power and dominion and every name that is named, not only in the present age, but also in the one to come.*

There is a spiritual war that involves every blood bought believer whether you believe it, act on it or engage in it or not. The spiritual war began in the heavens long before creation was spoken. The sanctified soul has been given the right of access by authority supernatural power through the death, burial and resurrection of Jesus Christ by the Spirit of Life through the way of the Cross to wage war against the Kingdom of darkness and to declare what is already ours. Yes! Casting, pulling down, releasing and making known in the earth realm the Kingdom laws in the heavenly courts taking back what belongs to you as an heir. The Seed of Christ, members of the Body of Christ, enemies of the devil and his work overcome through the Resurrected Power of Christ Jesus. We must draw, cling and chase after the Lord. He promises to draw nearer to us ready to avenge our cases and release our blessings. We must engage in the spiritual war by the Holy Spirit as they are called for through honesty, renunciation, denunciation, repentance, knowledge, prayer, deliverance, fasting, commitment, studying the word, worship and meditation, faithfulness, confession and the wisdom of GOD.

We must be aware of any door that is attempting to swing open through a simple conversation, dreams or thoughts. The entrance of all that opposes GOD should be cast down in the Name of Jesus because a stronghold can be formed over time if not cast down as the Lord commands through the Apostle Paul. Dark thoughts, imaginations can set off frequencies in the realm of the spirit. When they are dark they will draw the dark. *The Word of GOD declares in Proverbs 14:12 {NIV} There is a way appears to be right (to man), but in the end it leads to death.* When one thinks wrong long after a period of time, wrong will sound and look right and what is right will sound and look wrong. This has been a plot of Satan since the garden. We can recognize it for what it really is; a bait. If these chemically provoked energy cells are nourished they can inversely cause negative unnatural behavior patterns to arise with intent to control by growing in strength. This is one way something very small enlarges itself in time with manifestations. How? Through the unnatural root generated by darkness that is channeled through an open mindset of contrary desires and affections. Allure is the rule of attraction. We are like magnets in the dimension of the spirit realm. GOD who created attraction understands the Law of Attraction and has given the church principles to be governed by in the earth realm. Satan interfered with God's creative order; but the SEED of the woman, Yeshua HaMashiach *(Jesus Christ)* has disarmed and reversed the cycle of death and defeat by the Governing Power of Holy Spirit. Therefore, through our divine nature in Christ we will walk in the blessings of obedience and attract the hand of blessings; The Hand of Yahweh.

Satan's domain of authority and power is darkness. He hates the LIGHT and the TRUTH! He hates Yahweh, His Christ and Holy Spirit!

He hates all who represents and are carriers of the mark of the True Light sealed by Ruach Hakodesh. Darkness is darkness with no barriers or favoritism. It seeks out to send darts, strife, division and animosity to initiate hatred which is linked to murder, racism, family chaos and sibling rivalry. Also along with carnal jealousy, strife to occupy homes, division in marriages, government and twisting the truth so the Truth itself will be offensive to receive. Darkness divides parent-child relationships, bring confusion to the sexes, delusion, killing church fellowship, church growth, division among leadership and killing the vision of the Church whose vision is of Holy Spirit. Satan will send his messengers concealed as light to sow demonic seeds in any ministry for its downfall, setup discord among friendship, children and family and with all sort of genetic emptiness. Every shade of darkness *(nothingness)* originates from its source, the father of lies, who was a liar from the beginning; the unnatural strand of the evil genetic code that is absent of Light, absent of the Truth, absent of Holy Conviction, absent of Holiness and absent of Love authority and power is broken off those that believe.

Regardless of one's rank in life, status, race, creed or age we all bleed red blood and were born with a fallen nature. All sin is as scarlet and all souls are in need of total redemption provided through the Supernatural Governmental System of the Redeemer who lives today. And because Yeshua- *JESUS* lives those who respond to Him also shall have everlasting life and life abundantly in victory through severing the umbilical cord of worldliness. ***The Word of the LORD says come now consider your options, let us settle the matter, you can become white as wool {Isaiah 1:18}.*** Divine deliverance for the lost soul, the backslider and the Church supplement is the Lord's heart; His Way, His Bread and His Substance are always available to a repentant heart account.

As we take a scope look at the Genesis account we'll see the seed *(an offspring altered)* which is a spiritual genetic encoded mutation from the evil one against Elohim. Elohim's masterpiece was affected. Of all

Hidden comes from the Greek word **Kruptos**
• To conceal
• Lay up, hide
• Safety place
• Secret things (inward new nature)

of Yahweh's creation man is the only creature created in the Creator's image with the ability to conduct Yahweh's business in the earth. This speaks volumes in the realm of the spirit indicating every believer's divine abilities, position, identity and future. Our new life is declared already hidden in Christ *{Colossians 3:3-4}* not in self, not in our parents or grand-parents, jobs, materialism, the world or idols. This means to be united, crucified with the death of Christ and raised in safety, preserved and secure with the divine seal of guarantee in Yeshua the Christ.

Yahweh is Omniscience, Omnipresent and Omnipotent. He exists within Himself and makes covenant with Himself. In Him exists no darkness! No corruption exists in Him! No compromise exists in Him! No cunningness exists in Him! No double standard exists in Him! No perversion exists in Him! No rebellion, No bondage, No defeat exists in Him! No deception! No lies! No temptation! No deadly addictions! No accusation exists in Him! No mixed emotions! No failure! No confusion! No mixture! And No struggles exist in Him! But fire exists in Him! Everything that begins has a starting point and a source in order to shape its image and is produced by a seed, a thought, and an image with a declared word of authority to create upon. On the other hand, Yahweh's kingdom exists by complete supernatural order, wealth, righteousness, peace, joy, holiness, justice and love.

Lord, let every lame area of my life be healed,
and let me leap like a deer. Let my ears be open,
and every deaf area of life be unstopped.
Let every parched area of my life
become a pool and every
thirsty area of my life a
spring of water.

Isaiah 35:5-7

3

GENESIS ACCOUNT

* Let's look at the scriptures to bring clarity and insight on what is unfolding.

Genesis 2

V7 And the LORD God formed man of the dust of the ground and breathed into his nostrils the breath of life; and man became a living soul. **V9** And out of the ground made the Lord God to grow every tree that is pleasant to sight, and good for food; and the tree of life also in the midst of the garden, and the tree of knowledge of good and evil. **V15** and the LORD God took the man and put him into the Garden of Eden to dress it and to keep it.

Genesis 2

V27 So Yahweh Elohim created man in his image, in the image of Yahweh created he him; male and female created he them. **V28** And God blessed them and said unto to them Be fruitful and multiply and replenish the earth and subdue it: and have dominion over the fish of the sea, over the fowl of the air, over every living thing that move upon the earth. **V29** And God said, behold, I have given you every herb bearing seed, every tree, in which is a fruit of a yielding seed; to you it shall be for meat. **V30** And to every beast of the earth and to every fowl of the air and to everything that creepeth upon the earth wherein there is life, I have given every green herb for meat and it was so. **V31a** And Yahweh-Elohim saw every thing that he had made, and, behold, it was very good.

Genesis clearly details the divine chemistry of creative order in creation *{Genesis 1:1}*. However, verse 2 reveals a catastrophic chemical force where unnatural spiritual DNA was genetically and chemistry declined in a fall described as Satan being dethroned, cast down as falling like lightning from heaven *{Luke 10:1}*. This verse exposes the revelatory description of the essence of this realm's identity. These two words **formless** and **void** symbolically represent an atmospheric territory that breathes emptiness, confusion, futility, disorder, meaningless arguments, nothingness and wretchedness. The fall initiated the unfolding void of the kingdom of Satan, the satanic demonic realm that did not exist until that time. Yet, in the beginning confirms all accreditation that our Creator, the Author of life, is none other than Elohim, who spoke the foundation by His Logos. The Author of Life Himself provokes its beginning and its welfare to be sustained by His Glory for the existence in the full radiance of Himself. I repeat, "To exist in the fullness of YESHUA."

In the book of Genesis, Holy Spirit unveils the spiritual meaning of SEED. **In the Beginning** *(the Head -ROSH in Hebrew)* which means a birth, origin or source. The divine revelation of DNA coding speaks clearly through *Dabar Elohim* which is a hebraic title meaning the Spoken Word of God's breath. Yahweh-Elohim already had a master design in mind to formulate ADAM DNA. This lineage of one race would have the inborn nature of GOD. When GOD said, "Let **Us** make man in **OUR** image after **OUR** likeness," Adam's *(Eve)* total life support depended and relied upon the immeasurable unsubstantial radiance of Yahweh, Yeshua and the Ruach *(Godhead-triune)* who are **One** *{Colossians 1:9}* with distinctive personalities and roles. Thus far, we know according to scripture that outside of GOD is where chaos, anything unnatural, emptiness, worthlessness, confusion and non-existence are birthed from. GOD sees and calls it nothingness because it is completely destructive and void of all Truth and all Light. The unnatural, spiritually speaking, is governed by the demonic host. The SEED *(sperma)* Ruach *(Hebrew: Breath, Wind, Spirit- Greek: Pneuma)* DNA carried the sperma gene that made Adam and the Creator one in Spirit, **one** in form, **one** in soul, **one** in body and **one** in thought. **One!** The Spirit of GOD enveloped Adam in His Shekinah Glory. Adam although he was made from the dust of the ground his mind's capacity functioned in the same Glory as the Creator, which placed him in dimensions as a creator, but on a lower scale. The Spirit *(Wind of GOD)* rules as King from within. Dwelling in the Secret Place of the Most High releases magnetic attractions to believers filling our vessels with rivers of living water that will flow in areas of our daily lives. When we are ushered into the Glory, GOD reveals and delegates His thoughts, His knowledge, His wisdom toward us. Things that we may struggle with such as: guidance, patience, loving, singleness of mind, living a holy single life, how to be complete and single, how to achieve goals, overcome challenges, where to open my business, what to do in a marriage crisis, who to connect with, where to be planted or where do I go from here. The revelations are located in His Presence. The Presence gives us knowledge that we didn't obtain on our own. The Presence gives the worshiper divine wisdom, holy boldness and purity. The Presence is the divine portal that makes the transaction available. The Presence releases divine connections we hope for, but lack the information or resource. The Presence releases divine insight, strength, healing and deliverance to many souls who enter in. The Power of the Glory lights a fire to the soul. God's Glory is transforming. You cannot remain the same when entering His Presence wholeheartedly. Change will take place affecting the total you; a one on one personal encounter with your heavenly Father. The void in man's spirit did not exist until free will was stirred. As you yield yourself and stay in the intimate place of worship with GOD the mind of the flesh will be consumed and crucified. But when we are out of the place of worship the mind of the flesh rises and the law that is in the flesh will desire to rule you; the law of sin. The Presence is essential to every believer's new life and contentment.

The unnatural dwelling in a soul is known as the sinning or sinful carnality or carnal mind. And the sinful or fallen nature which came into existence through the process of the fall without divine order is prey to the lust of the flesh and pride of life. As the Church begins to understand the divine revelation of Truth and the Glory that is bestowed upon each soul raised with Christ by the Ruach of GOD and understand the inheritance of The LORD that pre-existed before the foundation of the worlds, the Ekklesia will then experience the full spiritual awareness and recognize its true nature's identity. Our identity in Christ carries volume in the realms. This is not just mere talk, this is reality. The mind is a realm. The body is a realm as well. We are heirs with Christ! Since heirs, we are beneficiaries of the Kingdom of Light whose King is clothed in the Shekinah Glory DNA. Believers are entitled to the kingdom's prosperity, its rank and have received by faith the inherent measure of the Glory of GOD as inheritors through the Spirit of Christ. *The Word of GOD declares in Roman 8:17 And if children, then heirs; heirs of God, and joint-heirs with Christ; if so be that we suffer with* **him,** *that we may be also glorified together.* A portion of the eternal inheritance grace birthright is for the community of faith to experience its reality on this side. Adam *(Eve)* demonstrates to the church the faith dimensions the believer can rise to when remaining in true fellowship with The LORD and also how deep a soul can fall outside of the supernatural divine will of God's Grace and Truth through unbridled free will. *However, the Word of GOD declares in Proverbs 24:16 A just man falls seven times and rises up again; but the wicked shall fall into mischief.* There is nothing that can prevent the just from getting back in their rightful place with GOD, **but self.** Because we know that our help comes from the LORD. As we lift the eyes of our heart to the source the soul is restored.

Everything GOD created still has divine purpose. And all that He created had a common commitment which was to worship. Adam *(Eve)* were a creative masterpiece with purpose which was to commune, fellowship in His Presence, rule, reign, cultivate, multiply and be fruitful in paradise. Adam's *(Eve)* direct frequency of language connected him with Yahweh and through Holy Spirit each believer has this frequency. The frequency is the channel for all activation and impartations as stated above. This sphere was all Adam inhaled and exhaled. Remember, all that is outside of the Light of GLORY does not exist in GOD nor share in His GLORY. However, under His tent is mercy and compassion with benefits extended to all open hearts. GOD holds no fellowship, intercourse or intimacy *(true spiritual worship)* with unholy allegiances or darkness. The Son of Jehovah *(Yahweh)* put on flesh and blood and paid the price of restitution for fallen nature by dying to redeem, purify and rescue us from yokes of bondage, chains of darkness, rebellion and perversion through His Blood, the supernatural DNA. After a soul admits their fall the first step to activate is acknowledging the sin or offense through the convicting influence of Holy Spirit who brings a deep heartfelt sorrow that leads to change, confession and turning from sins and throwing off weights. Then, applying the Blood of YESHUA to our conscience, our mind and our soul by faith for the complete process of total deliverance from the power and the practice of sin(s). As the believer continues to draw to the fountain and walk near to GOD in holiness, **the Blood** will forever cleanse and lift up a hedge of protection; never to lose its power of substance. Yeshua, the Ultimate Sacrificial Lamb of Yahweh, made the exchange through His life, body, death and resurrection for any soul that will come sincerely to Him for **complete** hope and salvation, **complete** wisdom and knowledge, **complete** guidance and strength, **complete** forgiveness and deliverance and **complete** love and welfare. *The Word of GOD declares in 1 John 1:5b God is Light and in Him there is no darkness at all.* GOD sees His offspring in the future state of being whole, made perfect in the Spirit of Christ. Therefore, walk in the process of innovation. He's in the business of the new mind elevation and soul renovation.

It is a devised corrupt system of illegal technicality from the created angel that felled from glory *(Lucifer)*. Satan who knows the future of the saints plants seeds of deceptive persuasion in order to cause division, isolation, spiritual and natural death over a course of time; subscribing to the imagination where thinking and reasoning is processed. This immaterial act materialized infusing the free will of man to over-power the voice of his Creator. Hereby taking the crown through the awaking of the fleshly appetite unrestrained senses. This is an attempt to remove the power of the True Light and to keep destiny from developing in the hearts, minds and souls of many. Darkness ignores and avoids Light. The subtlety factor of Satan is parallel to his fall, a destructive cunning system. The dragon called the devil along with his angels that where under his deceptive charismatic spell and power of persuasion was cast out of heaven down to the earth *{Revelation 12:7-9}*. The accuser's evil purpose is to target believers for a pitfall because he knows his time is short. The devil wants to ruin the Church's image and wipe us out; but he's already defeated. The Devil Is A Liar And the Truth Is Not Found In Him nor Can It Be!

In the transition of the fall the infinite spiritual DNA gene in Adam was altered and the Glory was hidden in order to keep from destroying Adam. Sin cannot stand in the Presence of GOD *{1 Corinthians 6:9; Revelation 21:27}*, just as darkness does not exist *{1John 1:5}*. When one is living or practicing sin, the same as being in darkness, good is not distinguished immediately, but we all no right from wrong; unless the conscience become seared. In the Presence of Yahweh, the Father, justice for all sin deserves the death penalty *{Leviticus chapter 20}.* But grace -favor not deserved-was in the essence of Yahweh according to His plan of justice. Yahweh's unconditional love is demonstrated and clothed in grace which manifests on behalf of human flaws of imperfection. When the crown of dominion had been spiritually and physically removed it affected Adam's means of physical and spiritual survival which affected the soul, the mind, the heart, the blood and the body. This means what once belonged to him by birthright was stripped. The keys, the glory, access, excellence, immortality, dominion, vision, the heavenly sphere and the authority, which determined a catastrophic change to be suitable for Adam's demoted physical and spiritual chemistry reaction of his total being. The poisoned knowledge received by them from the tree of the knowledge of good and evil penetrated every brain cell, nerve cell, atom and all other functions the human body and life would be in relation to and including the cosmic world. Therefore, the cosmic relocation of ADAM had to be provided for earthly *(mortal)* existence. The devil stole mankind's birthright inheritance to function as Kings *(no gender-position in God)* in order to keep mankind from knowing the code of who he or she really is as sons *(no gender-state of position)* of GOD: what our true estate is in GOD, our worth in Christ and to keep us from abiding in the Presence. The condemned mutation seed induced and brought on a spiritual transfer-reaction seen in the chart *(italicized words)* below. Faith acceptance through the Blood reverses curses. Every soul has to give account for their actions before the Supreme Justice Court of GOD. Because it is personal, if a soul consciously locates himself in any criminating negligent area, I implore you to measure your mind and heart condition by the WORD. Repent and receive the Grace of God's Love In Christ *{John 3:16-21}.*

• From mercy to *judgment*
• From favor to *guilt*
• From purity to *impurity*
• From rich to *poor*
• From worshiper to a *sinner*
• From faith to *fear*
• A desire for light rather than *darkness*
• From liberty to *bondage*
• From soberness to *rebellion*

In the Heavenly Kingdom Court of Yahweh-Elohim the enemy presented the technicality in the Presence of Yahweh-Elohim bringing charges that ADAM *(God called them Adam)* disobeyed His command that was attached to severe consequences. The commandment had a promise of judgment for disobedience and blessings for obedience attached to it. The accuser will appear about you to GOD just as he appeared in the Presence of the LORD with the sons of God. They appeared in the Lord's Presence for there assignments to be released from the Kingdom Courts of Yahweh concerning Joshua *{Zechariah 3:1}. The Word of GOD declares in Job 1:6 Now there was a day when the sons of God came to present themselves before the LORD, and Satan came also among them.* This revelation is how he goes to and fro to seek whom he may devour before the Judge concerning your soul's estate. The devil will bring charges up against anyone, especially those of the household of faith.

When we are in Christ, the testing of our faith, which is a distinguishing substance that points to our identity and function, will be on trial. It's never about us directly, but about the position we hold in Christ, the Anointed One. However, GOD will use the ugly, the bad and the good to bring us up to another dimension of faith, build godly character and cultivate our identity in Him. ABBA loves to see Himself in His children. The reflection will always tell the truth. The devil does not want us to know who we really are and what power you really possess in the earth. Satan wants the believer to focus on self and being human. That's deception in the eyes of GOD. We are created in the image of GOD that puts an end to Satan's lie. Therefore, the redeemed of the Lord bears a portion of glory through the salvation and the resurrection of our new life in Christ. When your heart and mind conducts you through the power of the Holy Spirit to abide, walk, talk, live and behave in your GOD-gene you become sensitive to sin and a weapon of threat to the kingdom of darkness and Satan knows it. It's working for the believers greater good. And if you fall, acknowledge the sin, take responsibility, shake yourself, repent, don't wallow, don't pretend or rehearse it, but start afresh in JESUS Name. The Blood, likened unto hyssop, has already completed the work and The Living Word -JESUS- is our deliverer and the Holy Spirit our teacher. Remember, our weapons are spiritual. They are supernatural sanctioned and ordained of GOD. Discerning of spirit is one of the gifts of the Ruach Hakodesh for any believer. GOD said, you have not because you ask not. Asking amiss or with the wrong motive will hinder the manifestation of the gift's demonstrative power and impartation. The gift is holy and it's from Holy Spirit. The vessel cannot bare bitter and sweet water at the same time. This gift helps the believers pray effective heart felt prayers according to the Spirit of GOD and not according to the cravings or dictations of the flesh. This gift even helps believers to determine who the source behind our visions and dreams is and how to interpret them. If you are saved and in right standing with GOD, earnestly seek and ask Holy Spirit to fill you and activate the gift of discernment of spirits *{1 Corinthians 12:10}.*

CONFESSION

When a believer walks in habitual sin, disobedience and does not **repent** of that wicked thing done, big or small; bearing the wrong fruit, then judgment from the righteous Judge will be established according to Yahweh's Court Justice. However, true repentance is an inward change with evidence of its fruitfulness of a changed mind of perfection established in Christ, perfecting of the soul in true light; washing that blemish spotless in the WORD. This is fruit that is evident of change; it's noticeable in the content of character. Do not give our adversary legal grounds or access to your mind to present a case against you. Confess all **unconfessed** sins, faults and shut down all accusations that can be used against you in the Divine Kingdom Court of Law. True confession breaks down walls and destroys pride. It's like a hammer in the realm of the spirit, crushing stones using them as stepping stones rather than stepping over them. It becomes a stepping stone for revelatory experience and progress advancement. This may also mean going to any person or people that you may have offended or holding guilty and **genuinely, sincerely** ask them to forgive you. Ask them to forgive you for your words or actions toward them and bring closure. It's no shame, but liberation when we can ask another person to forgive us even when we haven't purposely done anything or is aware that we have done something and whole heartily mean it. This is humility at work. When there is a fault against another the believer is responsible and accountable to GOD and that person to set the course right in love and truth regardless if they receive it or not. When we are hidden in Christ, Jesus is the one stepping up and the mind of the flesh and its deeds is bowing down in submission. Jesus tells believers by this all men shall know that you are my disciples that you exemplify love toward one another *{John 13:34-34}*. Yeshua HaMashiach advanced His workmanship of love through us to an extended arena. Jesus commands us to love our enemies and those whom we feel have wronged us *{Matthew 5:44}*. This will call for a deep heart examination, dying to self, battling the war within self, prayer, willingness, submission, faith and obedience. GOD is Great All the Time! We have a great intercessor *(high priest and attorney)* who is more that capable of pleading our case before Yahweh, the Father, and the Blood of Yeshua is not defiled. There is no sin or burden too great or to small that **His Blood** cannot actively **purge**. Yeshua's blood rectifies the guilt and shame of a true worshiper reaching the lowest valley and hidden chambers of the heart! *The Word of GOD declares in Romans 8:34 Who is he that condemns? It is Christ that died, yea rather, that is risen again, who is even at the right hand of God, who also makes intercession for us, the true worshipers.* The persecutor, Satan, has no charge when our shame *(result of the guilt)* and guilt are forgiven, purged and washed by Yeshua's Blood never to be bought up again. GOD said, that He will not remember the sin as far as the east is to the west nor shall you rehearse it.

- *The Word of GOD declares in Psalm 103:11-12 For as the heaven is high above the earth, so great is his mercy toward them that fear him. As far as the east is from the west, so far hath he removed our transgressions from us.*

- *he Word of GOD declares in Isaiah 43:25 I, even I, am he that blotted out thy transgressions for mine own sake, and will not remember thy sins.*

There is no one likened unto Yahweh, Daddy. Therefore, you shall not harbor any past sins in your heart nor walk in deceit, but complete liberation in mind, soul, spirit and body through the Power of the Blood of Yeshua *(JESUS)*. *The Word of GOD declares in Romans 8:1-2 There is therefore now no condemnation to them which are in Christ Jesus, who walk not after the flesh, but after the Spirit. For the law of the Spirit of life in Christ Jesus hath made me free from the law of sin and death.* If one has not truly repented of sin there will be a case presented before the Holy One concerning your guilt in the court of Heaven. *The Word of GOD declares in Isaiah 43:26 {Holman} Take me to court; let us argue our case together, state your case, so that you maybe vindicated.* Remember, there is no failure in GOD, because He lives within your heart there shall be no grudges or deceit found in your temple. When GOD forgives He forgets. It's erased from the spiritual account of that soul. Only that soul can allow that evil to reverse itself. This should encourage us to repent and reflect ABBA-Daddy's essence in character, because forgiveness is an attribute of Father GOD that is in the believer's DNA GOD-gene. The fruit does not fall far from the tree. Guilt and shame are unholy fruit of the work of iniquity and transgression. These are fruit belonging to Satan's kingdom sphere of darkness. The curse of the fall ushered in the side of Yahweh's holiness that is formed in judgment against all unrepented sin, transgression and iniquity. Yeshua the Christ is Holy and Righteous full of Light and Splendor. All sin has to be judged according to His Justice and divine order. Remember, the evil spiritual encoding passed its abnormal, diverted spiritual genetic gene into the spirit of mankind. Satan, the crafty trickster, has been planning the perversion of the image, purpose and true identity of mankind from that time even until now.

The Tree of Life

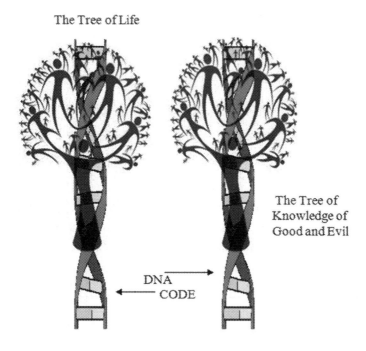

The Tree of
Knowledge of
Good and Evil

DNA
CODE

- *Seed: offspring; sperma*

- *DNA: transcript; house genetic information*

- *Chromosomes: Chroma (color), Soma (body) patterns of light and dark*

- *Genetics: Codes passed on when organisms reproduce.*

Genesis 3

V4 And the serpent said unto the woman Ye shall not surely die: **V5** For God do know that in the day ye eat thereof, then your eyes shall be opened and ye shall be as gods, knowing good and evil. **V6** And when the woman saw that the tree was good for food, and that it was pleasant, and a tree to be desired to make one wise, she took of the fruit thereof and did eat and gave unto her husband with her and he did eat. **V15** And I (God) will put enmity between thee and the woman and between thy seed and her seed, it shall bruise the head and thou shall bruise thy heel. **V21** Unto Adam also and to his wife did the LORD God make coats of skins and clothed them. **V24a** So he drove out man; and placed at the east of the garden of Eden Cherubims, and a flaming sword which turned every way, to guard the way of the tree of life.

The soul of fallen man is lost and condemned without the regeneration of the Spirit of Christ who gives the ability and influence to live. When GOD created man in His image, male and female, He created them; the divine creative order of DNA was genetically infused into Adam's being. Elohim breathed in and Adam became a living being. What did Yahweh-Elohim breathe? Yahweh-Elohim breathed His Spirit into hard-formed lifeless dust, creating His likeness through dust and that dust became a divine endless life. That mold of clay had on it Yahweh's full Glory and Spirit inwardly. The Glory is extremely significant in its manifestation and powerful. The Glory carries the attributes, hidden mysteries, vision and will in immeasurable depths of Light. This level of Glory can transform, as well as, destroy. Moses and Isaiah had testimonials of this infinite electrical charge that transformed their very countenance and inner quality of being that people could not handle their presence because of the GLORY that engulfed them as a consequence of being before the Shekinah Glory Presence. Yahweh's Glory is another title description of His form, principle and function of Himself in Spirit-form.

Hebrew term for Glory
Hod: Kabod: weight or heaviness, presence
Greek term for Glory
Doxa: brightness, splendor, judgment, value, honor

Yahweh-Elohim had declared all that he had created was very good with moral excellences. There was no separation, flawless; no flaws, no evil, no perversion and no sin until chapter three when the intruder, the tempter, made his appeal through the serpent. The tempter with his method of spiritual molestation ushered in a diabolic shift into the atmosphere, in the soul of Adam and in the Covenant fellowship -bond between Adam and Yahweh. Now this isn't just a deception only, but a setup for division, breaking of covenant, alienation and recruitment from the devil. A spiritual plot through a defiled word planted in the imagination giving birth to a lie from the father of lies. A defiled thought creating a vain imagination that painted a picture of what seemed to have looked innocent in image and sound harmless to the fleshly appetite, a thought; yet, to deceive the innocent and begin his own defective spiritual posterity line in the earth. This death cycle is only destroyed through the finished work of the Cross; the death, the burial and the resurrection of Christ Jesus. This spermicidal genetic seed began a cycle that will only be terminated, destroyed, wiped out and denounced through the Blood of Yeshua HaMashiach. The adulterous fall conceived and gave birth through the spirit of pride, the spirit of lust *(eyes-flesh)* and unbelief through the serpent's clever seduction, bewitching and hypnotized tactics. This spiritual act of perversion which interrupted the supernatural divine nature *(DNA)* of Yahweh-Elohim's covenant-bond with his creation would affect EVERYTHING and ALL THINGS in creation. However, Yahweh's love expanded ahead of creation and time for the **deliverance** and **grace** and divine **government** to prevail against all wickedness for the new structuring. In the fullness of time, His love and compassion is accessible now and until the end of time to anyone who chose the way of life through Christ the Messiah.

Due to fallen Adam *(Eve)*, the universe and the totality of man's being- spirit, soul, mind and body- is now contaminated with shame, guilt, rebellion, perversion, transgression, sin, judgment and the curse which entered the physical realm affecting creation as a whole. All that was created by the Ruach of our Creator, Yahweh-Elohim, was reduced to spiritual aberration. The depravity, falsehood, perjury, trespass, iniquities, death, hostility, alienation, broken fellowship with the LORD and caused a loss in His Glory Estate. Even though Yahweh gave them the first law of command in the garden with conditions, He had already forethought provision for the fulfillment of the grace-code dispensation in kairos time that symbolically pointed to the Yeshua *(JESUS- Yahweh Is Salvation)* HaMashiach *(Messiah)*. He gave them the freedom or the free will during a probationary period when one would be entitled to choose life or death and because of their free will outside of GOD, disobedience was activated. Yet, the LORD alone searches for any heart that will come out of their despondent condition by answering the call of the divine rehabilitation through grace for new life. ***The Word of GOD declares in John 6:63 It is the spirit that quicken (make alive); the flesh profit nothing: the words that I speak unto you, they are spirit, and they are life.***

Lord, let me be delivered out of the hand of my
enemies, and let me serve You without
fear, in holiness and righteousness,
all the days of my life.

Luke 1:74-75

4

THE BLOOD, THE SPIRIT

The Blood and the Spirit have mutual purposes in common: its mobility of life and the flowing river of life; both give life. When you think of the natural bloodline of humanity, what images do you envision? In the natural sense we understand the bloodline is the source that can link parenthood or progeny, siblings and trace family lineage from generation to generation. Channeled information can be gathered from blood that reveals what possibly may be in the bloodline, such as, sickness, disease, drugs, alcohol and blood type. The blood is mobile and it moves throughout the entire body supplying nourishment and moving waste out. And the line of the blood is that which can link each individual to their race, family, heredity, patterns, cycles and the most interesting of all is the nature. The nature in the bloodline yokes us to our personality, character and spirit. And without blood nothing can be traced, transferred or received from the line of blood. The human body carries blood throughout our system for transporting signals, oxygen, purifying, removing toxin, regulating and stabilizing and for all the involuntary and voluntary functions of the human body. Some of these functions portray a spiritual pattern of what occurs by the work of the Spirit of GOD. Study shows that the natural blood consists of plasma, white blood cells, red blood cells and platelets, etc. These are DNA coded to carry vital information to and from organs and other major parts of the human body for its proper functioning. If the blood source shuts down the human organs will cease in operating as they were designed. Therefore, defections *(defects, defilement)* that may develop through the blood, whether at birth or through open doors over-time can pass through the genes in the bloodline. Some genes lay dormant and produce cell growth when they are nourished.

When opposition, fleshly carvings and the voice of the evil approach you, you must be able to stand against the tricks and schemes of evil's deception. And this is not easily done when ears are dull or eyes are blind to truth or the hearts are callous by the winds of change due to what life has been presented in your path, whether through influence or bloodline. ***The Word of GOD declares in James 4:7 Submit yourselves therefore to God. Resist the devil, and he will flee from you.*** There are steps a believer must engage toward in order to face your foe and remove the blockage. The first step in deliverance is to admit where your heart and mind is in order to release the Hand of GOD that delivers the healing and the power for the soul. Divine wisdom, understanding and knowledge are spiritual gifts for walking in the divine creative order that Elohim established. Our strength, our power, our own understanding and brain power has no impact or power to deliver us from ourselves. Nor can it bring deliverance, break curses, break familiarity or break sin's authority and power. The only way is by the Power of the Blood of Yeshua that our spiritual diseases in our bloodline *(lifeline)* are healed.

The world in itself was not created evil, but evil made its entrance into the world, causing the chemistry to change the atmospheric realms. Mostly that which has been labeled tainted, defiled, defeated, sinful, evil, unclean, unholy and impure can be restored, purged, justified, sanctified and acquitted of all allegations and judgments through the Gate, YESHUA. He is the only **Door** that GOD the Father has given access back to Him for all souls to be restored, rescued and reformed *{John 14:6}*. The new birth is supernatural, not natural. When there is an understanding of what Truth is, walking in our new nature will become like second skin; natural and expected. Then, believers should expect the supernatural, think the supernatural and work the supernatural. It's the believer's wealth inheritance. Yeshua HaMashiach's Life, Blood and Spirit are **One**, the DNA antidote that supplies the inner cleansing of total spiritual defection and forms a bloodline protection for kingdom citizens against the viral plagues that appear to wage a war generationally in the bloodline in the spirit and mind of souls. Healing is a beneficial gift from ABBA that is always available for all who seek to be healed. Although it's Already done, you want to see the full manifestation of what is **Already** promised to you. Souls do not have to stay sick, spiritually broke, when healing is free, but one must be knowledgeable of their need of a physican. Just as the human blood flows and works with multi-cell delivery in the body system is a shadow of how the Blood of Yeshua delivers; even with greater purpose of working for the spiritual condition of the spirit of the mind. We understand that blood is part of the human physical DNA needed in the earth's sphere which consists of cells, neutrons, chromosome patterns, protons, electrons, molecules and such like traits for the natural state. The Incarnate Christ -God in the flesh- was human and divine. He reversed the curse, indignation and death cycles and destroyed the works of the evil one through His purity and uncontaminated blood. Yeshua provided life for all who surrender, repent, believe, obey and walk with Him continually.

The human issues of personal life that many of us experience saved or not saved, good or evil, in the church and in families comes down the same spiritual path and logic. The problems that arrest the spirit are spiritual problems; even though the outcome is manifested, it is spiritual. These conditions are released from the individual spirit and their imagination directed from within, without and can affect others through persuasion. The key to remember is that the physical condition at hand has arrived because of the condition of a soul spiritual state with JESUS is detached or not whole in that area of the spirit of the mind. That informs us that Christ *(Messiah-Lord)* wants to flow with full access to all of you, in every way. He wants to be Lord in every door and chamber in your mind and heart. Holy Spirit doesn't invade where a block or off limit sign is posted. Letting the guard down is a personal submission role. GOD knows the issues of the heart that you are dealing with and He knows the matters of the heart that haven't entered the mind; yet He wants to flow inwardly to set up His DNA code to prevent and block the plans of the adversary. Let Him completely in the door to dress you properly within. When we are spiritually dressed properly it covers the physical situations as well. It's in the bloodline of Yeshua that draws the line with decrees that spiritual emptiness and failure shall not prevail, overrule or overcome the believer. The bloodline is like a line in the sand it has already declared that the case is settled. Therefore, stir the virtue and let the healing flow. Let It Flow! Even if a situation is in progress, grace in the form of the WORD which is a spiritual SEED has to be allowed to penetrate intimately into the soul for the restoration process of the Fire of Holy Spirit to burn out and burn in. It is the Power of the Blood and the Spirit that heals the wounded soul and stops the corrosion of the heart and its inner bleeding. Callousness and inner bleeding comes from piled up, suppressed hurt that refuses to let its fortress be torn down.

Satan, the author of confusion, instigates half truths to create confusion in the psyche arena that spreads like a wildfire to the soul. Some inner spiritual bleeding work in patterns or cycles within a soul, which means an unclean spirit can lie dormant until something triggers imbalanced cells to produce in order to protect its aggressive reasoning. Whether up or down, patterns are like a spin cycle, they rise every now and then; there could possibly be a dark presence behind the aggressive manifestation. Spin cycles of this magnitude may possibly be rooted back early as childhood or teen years from relationships or other factors. Whether its through holding on to hurtful words spoken to you, regrets of the pass, resentment, unwanted pregnancy, rape, molestation, divorce, physically or emotionally abused, abortions, dysfunctional family relationships, hurtful memories, maybe forced to do things that invaded you has an individual, called names that degraded you has a person, people lied on or about you or maybe the other way around or even taken advantage of by someone that supposed to have loved you. THE TRUTH IS GOD IS RELEASING HIS HEALING VIRTUE TO AN OPEN HEART AND MIND! ***WHATEVER IT IS, THAT PLAGUE MUST BOW ITS HEAD AND FLEE AT THE NAME OF JESUS!*** Whatever the case(s) may be, this is how deep defilements of the heart can linger on when a soul doesn't know how to let go, forgive, or release the pain, fail to forgive or harbors animosity. When seeds are planted and conceived in the mind they will intrude through the swinging door and other familiar spirits will fester in that heart until the issue is confronted and resolved. We know great minds think alike, but negative minds think alike also. It's energy. Good fruit and bad fruit each have a source. It doesn't spring up on its own. As the Spirit invades the soul changes take place spiritually and naturally. All that crosses the bloodline must be handled by the Spirit *not the flesh* and the Power of His WORD in prayer. That is the lifestyle stance in which the Church is to stand, fight and war from. In the pain or set backs, WAR! In tears, WAR! Rage, Revenge, WAR! Worry, WAR! Confusion, evil rising, WAR! In distress, WAR! Self-pity, WAR! Loneliness, WAR! Low self-worth, WAR! Lacking, WAR! Family deliverance, WAR! Flesh rise, WAR! Shake and saturate yourself in the Word of GOD. **"I Decree, The Chains of Limitations Break Off Your Mind and Spirit!"** This is the believer's dominion; take what belongs to you by force in the realm of the Spirit by pulling down these false altars that have been built in the mind and appear to look like giants in JESUS Name. The giant of holiness must rise from within your DNA in Christ. Our identity in Christ legalizes our righteous posture and heaven secures our back. We are the spiritual giants in Christ. *The Word of GOD declares in Judges 3:1-2 {NIV} Now these are the nations which the LORD left, to prove Israel by them, even as many as Israel as had not known all the wars of Canaan; Only that the generations of the children of Israel might know, to teach them war.*

The effects of the power of persuasion run deep spiritually, but can be uprooted and torn down through surrendering to the Will of

GOD. That means apply the Word, honor the Blood of JESUS and yield to the pruning of the Holy Spirit. When you see cliques whether, in the church, on the job, school or in the family the law of attraction is at work. Remember, sperma- *seed*, carries the attraction code of its giver for producing; the cycle repeats itself until it is stopped. What started as a seed will grow into a tree through the nourishment of unhealthy, unhealed emotions. However, if the tree *(soul)* is fruitful its growth is due to healthy nourishment. This seed bed is a breathing ground in any situation that spiritually and unknowingly is open to inviting spirits into the soul. Because that heart has opened itself up to believe and act on what has been presented, the devil assigns his demons to continually make demands on that soul, breaking down safe barriers in order to build a false fortress in the heart and mind that fortifies the pride of self indulgence and self knowledge. This is a process; it doesn't happen all at once. This is what happened to mother Eve. A stronghold fastened its grip to her mind and heart by having an entrance into her psyche. A dark presence has the ability to clothe any open unprotected soul. That dark spiritual genetic gene purposefully changes the essences of a person's inner and outer self. This brings on an identity crisis. Any identity confusion in appearance and character is not the will of the LORD. When a soul acknowledges they are in bondage deliverance can start at that moment, unlocking the mind and soul through application of the Eternal Word of GOD. We cannot say, Lord, help me and don't take the medicine or apply the principles that is the healing for the ailment in the mind. Lord, Help Me is a dying call to GOD to intervene with divine reinforcement and supernatural strength that overcomes us, like a cocktail shot. The soul and mind gets healed not worst. The devil's mission is canceled. We bounce out of that place of isolation. As a soul comes to the conclusion of reasoning that self is in need of divine help now and ready to receive from above, then the Master's touch can be experienced.

- *The Word of GOD declares in Isaiah 54:17 No weapon that is formed against me will prosper: and every tongue that shall rise against me in judgment thou shall condemn. This is the heritage of the servants of the LORD, and their righteousness is of me, saith the LORD.*

The devil's attack technique in the Garden dealt with the framework of logic plus action. The attack is never physical first, but it is always spiritual first and then promotes itself through probing minds that lack understanding, minds that are weary, easily offended, stubborn or open for new and instant gratification. Demons speak to minds and hearts just as Satan used the snake to prophesy a lie into Eve's life. And this lie targeted *(Adam)* Eve's identity and position of who she **already** was and what she **already** possessed. She was queen with eternal high rank authority; above darkness. She already had all the divine wisdom and divine knowledge that she ever needed. Mother Eve didn't realize or recognize the cloak she was clothed in. Why did she feel as if she needed to be enlightened outside of God's wisdom? The church must be alert, watchful, on guard and aware of this very same defection and deception. Especially, the new age movement that's attempting to force itself into the Body of Christ. BEWARE! The devil is using this same ideology against and within the Church today. The trickster has not changed, but is intensifying his attacks. True believers must be willing and ready to be trained by the Spirit in the WORD of GOD to discern the voice of the devil. He uses disguises and his approach doesn't appear as he is. He may be smooth with his tongue in some cases and roar like a roaring lion in others. Its not that thoughts won't voice themselves, but its when those accusations present themselves in action what action will you take to discern the spirit- voice manifesting through the person? We are instructed to be sober and watchful because the adversary, as a roaring lion, walk about seeking whom he may devour *{1 Peter 5:8}*. He cannot devour you when armed properly. The motive behind his seeking is to catch us weak and off focus. The Power of Christ is within you to master and overcome! It has been delegated to you and you have been given authorization. That's DNA Dominion! ***The Word of GOD declares in Ephesians 1:20 It's according to the power that works in you.*** The power influences through an active lifestyle of faith. ***The Word of GOD declares in John 10:27 My sheep listen (hear, know, recognize) my voice and they follow Me.*** Take a faith move and cover your eye gates with the Blood of Jesus, your eyes gates with the Blood of Jesus, your hand and mouth gates with the Blood of Jesus, your imagination with the Blood of Jesus, cover your family with the Blood of Jesus, your job, finances, your health, education, your going and coming, uprising and down sitting, your vehicle and its components and against all that appear to be wicked or harmful. Christ's DNA that lives in the soul of the believer gives believing believers the right of authority and power. The Blood of Jesus is the household of faith hedge of protection. ***The Word of GOD declares in Exodus 12:13 {NIV} The blood will be a sign to you on the houses where you are, and when I see the blood, I will pass over you. No destructive plague will touch you when I strike Egypt.***

Prayer

"I DECREE THAT I CONQUER ALL FALSE VOICES THAT SPEAK CUNNINGLY AND CLEVERLY; AND EVERY ACCUSATION AGAINST ME SHALL BE OVERTHOWN IN THE MATCHLESS NAME OF JESUS THE CHRIST AS I STAND UNDER THE BANNER OF LOVE AND VICTORY! I DECREE THAT MY DELIVERANCE BE MANIFESTED IN THE SPIRIT OF MY MIND! I DECREE MY HEART MELT UNDER THE FIRE OF GOD AND THE FIRE OF GOD SATURATES MY TOTAL BEING!" I GOT THE VICTORY IN JESUS!

Amen.

Faith has different measures, different dimensions, different results that access locations; Strong Faith, Weak Faith, Little Faith, Great Faith! Faith gives us the ability to do the will of the Father, but if one is not **In Christ** he is in the flesh. He cannot please the Father and lack the ability to do the will of the Father. Pastors or leaders cannot issue the gift of faith; it comes from the divine source of Holy Spirit's DNA. Yahweh is the originator of faith *{1Corinthians 12:9; Romans12:3-8; Ephesians 2:8}.* It is increased by the Holy Spirit as one personally walks in agreement, submit, commit and obey the instructions. Faith is an impartation from GOD to be **activated** in you. It's not in your -GOD gene- DNA to be defeated or abused or trampled on. Defeat, doubt and abuse can be conquered when four (4) factors are changed in heart and action that are not substances of the true Light and faith:

- Not knowing the truth!
- Not activating the truth!
- Not believing the truth!
- Knowing, but omitting the truth!

The DNA of the Blood of Yeshua HaMashiach *(Jesus the Christ-Messiah)* has **Already** triumphed over the world systems, elements of the world, the works of the flesh, iniquity, fear, defeat, generational curses and indictments that will rise against us. The Kingdom's priceless wealth and royalties have passed through the Blood of Christ to the Bride. It's Already Done! We have to initiate the principles by making it practical in our daily circumstances. Your soberness and loyalty permits you to walk in this sphere by faith and obedience canceling out all foreign voices of influence leading one astray and to cancel the appetite of sin. The complete finished work on the Cross at Calvary carried with it the Kingdom Promise. We are raised by way of the Cross from death to life and from defeat to victory. What Christ accomplished on the Cross at Calvary is made available to be fully occupied by the born-again believer and transferred through the supernatural umbilical cord of Holy Spirit and the Eternal Word into the believer's spiritual womb. The **Blood DNA** feeds, nourish, support, expose, execute, drives out, transport, supply and gives exceptionality and distinctiveness of the new image's sufficiency. *The Word of GOD declares in 2 Corinthians 12:9 {NIV} Yeshua tells us, My Grace is sufficient for you and my power is made perfect in weakness.* The Kingdom of GOD in Christ is set up for divine perfection to be evident in the earth realm through its royal citizens, the faithful ones. Just as an umbilical cord is the lifeline of the baby in the mother's womb, the Blood and the Spirit is the lifeline source of perfection for believers. As long as we sojourn in this land the Ruach Hakodesh *(Holy Spirit)* guarantees us the promise of safety. ABBA is our Father and the sons of GOD are the reflecting image of their biological daddy. Richness is guaranteed through Yeshua's **Blood and Spirit** with multi-benefits.

- *The Word of GOD declares in Ephesians 1:18-23 The eyes of your understanding being enlightened; that ye may know what is the hope of his calling, and what the riches of the glory of his inheritance in the saints, And what is the exceeding greatness of his power toward us who believe, according to the working of his mighty power, Which he wrought in Christ, when he raised him from the dead, and set him at his own right hand in the heavenly places, Far above all principality, and power, and might, and dominion, and every name that is named, not only in this world, but also in that which is to come: And hath put all things under his feet, and gave him to be the head over all things to the church, Which is his body, the fullness of him that fills all in all.*

<u>CURSES</u>

The heart is deceitful above all things and desperately wicked: who can know it? Understand that delusion and illusion are results of the image of fabrication. It bares no ground for truth to stand. Let's view the blood-line in a deeper perspective. I believe although things are in the bloodline which we have concluded may manifest through a door that is not guarded. These doors can open in the natural through spiritual wounds, hidden secrets of the heart and ongoing unresolved situations through minds that are void of accepting truth over self *(pride);* and what is fed by emotions to be accepted as natural and normal. Many may know it's not normal, but may feel trapped and want a way out without drawing attention to ones self; yet struggles within. And on the flip side of that coin, many accept these imaginations and emotion acts as being a part of what is called the norm. However, the seed of Satan ushered in a new world order. A curse can reign and have dominion through entrance of rebellious disobedient minds, stubbornness and unbelief *{Hosea 4:6}.* While blessings reign, rule and have dominion through submission-obedience faithful and repentant hearts. People sometimes unaware speak curses or harm over themselves. A curse can be described as a figure of speech, wish or an evil utterance of action with intension to inflict harm toward someone. Curses can backfire *{Numbers 22}.* They may be in a form of spoken words or in letter form. However, Yahweh GOD instructs us to bless and curse not *{Romans 12:14}.* A generational curse past through the bloodline through the spiritual umbilical cord that can only be severed by the Seed of Righteousness; the Blood of JESUS applied to the mind and heart. Curses are a result of the heart being continuously rebellious to GOD and unbelief; yet the LORD is loving, long suffering, compassionate and ready to reverse all curses from minds that will respond in faith and obedience *{Numbers 14:18; Exodus 20:5; Leviticus 26: 40-42}.* Generational curses may also come by the act of a choice that the mind and heart makes, but is not aware of the consequences that the decision is going to unlock. Even though a curse is the result of spiritual decline on another's end, it cannot cross the bloodline of the blood on the heart of those who are whole heartily in the will of the Father regardless of the life of that parent or fore parent or such *{Deuteronomy 5:8-10; 24:16}*. It cannot actively cross the bloodline of one that opposes the darkness it brings. Just because it appears in one's family don't mean one have to accept its force. That's the power of our DNA in Christ activated. ***The Word of GOD declares in Galatians 3:13b-14 Christ redeemed us from the curse of the law by becoming a curse for us, for it is written: CURSED IS EVERYONE WHO HANGS ON A TREE. He redeemed us in order that the blessings given to Abraham might come upon the Gentiles, so that by faith we might receive the promise of the Spirit.*** Spiritual genetic traits beyond sickness and disease of the body, such as, mean spirited, hatred, whoremonger, hyper-sexuality, incest, seduction, smoking, alcoholism, unbelief, lewdness, homosexuality, racism, idolatry, adultery, lying, trickery, greed, laziness, addictions, licentiousness, rage, filthiness, arrogance, manipulative and such like can pass from one generation to the next through this diabolic spiritual umbilical cord. One way this is discerned is when families have a repeat cycle from a generation before and walk in it time after time without understanding and spiritual awareness. Spiritual diseases pass with an underlying hidden code to seize the soul, to corrupt family identity, destroy and lay claim to that soul. Remember, the unseen spiritual world is not seen with the carnal or natural eye. It's only discerned by the Holy Spirit living in hearts of believers, taking up residence to empower *{1Corinthians 2:14; 12:10}*. GOD loves all and His grace is sufficient for All.

Listed below are Kingdom benefits of the Royal Bloodline that passes from the Heavenly Father's Estate through King Jesus- the Lion of Judah, to the Tribe of Judah- the believers hidden in Christ:

- The Bloodline of Yeshua position believers in the kingdom
- The Bloodline of Yeshua washes our sins away
- The Bloodline of Yeshua removes the guilt
- The Bloodline of Yeshua brings the peace of Yahweh
- The Bloodline of Yeshua protects and covers
- The Bloodline of Yeshua cancels out the old nature
- The Bloodline of Yeshua gives the new nature
- The Bloodline of Yeshua contains our spiritual blessings
- The Bloodline of Yeshua seals every Promise
- The Bloodline of Yeshua provides restoration
- The Bloodline of Yeshua cancels our debt
- The Bloodline of Yeshua releases healing virtue
- The Bloodline of Yeshua divides
- The Bloodline of Yeshua sets us free
- The Bloodline of Yeshua pronounces war and victory
- The Bloodline of Yeshua is the line of defense

The spirit of ignorance is a destroyer with no discrimination toward any soul. Knowledge is powerful when understood and activated. The kingdom of darkness will sift the life out of a soul, keep a soul's mind imprisoned and in fear. The paradigm, mind patterns, must shift. The spirit of fear differs from the Spirit of the fear of the Lord. The fear of the Lord causes the soul to react to the Lord in obedience and to His awe of greatness, power and love that has been shown toward thee. The spirit of fear paralyses anyone from growing and moving forward into their God-given call or destiny and the devil has known this from the beginning. The spirit of fear attempts and assails to lay hold of the mind from receiving light. The spirit of fear will shut you down and block out The Word of GOD. It persuades the spirit of man that there is no better way for them, just live life with what has been assessed to you from your own wisdom, hand and power and in your own strength; after all GOD is GOD. He understands and knows where you are. Just do you. That sounds so right, yet is not from the Spirit of Truth. Doing us outside of the Truth is our will and bowing the heart in submission to GOD is His will and our first love *{Proverbs 14:12}*.

That which passes through the bloodline is spiritually related. Issues can be transferred without warning or approval. Blood issues can show up in the genes. When a fetus is forming in the womb of the mother such things can enter in through the umbilical cord affecting the unborn infant emotionally, spiritually and physically in reality. The vital common key point is the transfer to the womb. A proven fact is when a parent has been on drugs those drugs can travel to the unborn infant with the possibilities of affecting that child with a pre-addiction appetite, congenital issues, as well as, emotional and behavioral issues. When parents have deep emotionally ups and downs, illicit sexual behavior, alcohol, anger issues, nicotine and/ or any addiction or behavioral issues these traits can pass to the innocent unborn child who had no say in the matter, but was violated of their human innocence and molested spiritually. Sometimes issues can lay idle and later develop in the person's teen or adult years. When this happens it triggers unusual attitudes and/ or behavior in the individual. This is another form in which spiritual doors can become opened and issues of the blood can travel through the birth canal undetected by the natural eye. Therefore, the case calls for the Cross, the Blood of Yeshua. Yeshua, our salvation, preserves us from evils diseases and falsities; being nothing but spiritual diseases. Evils and falsities strip health away from the internal portion of man, induce sicknesses in the mind and illnesses in the body. A healthy mind, a healthy spirit and a healthy soul helps to promote a healthy body out weighing the bad. The DNA GOD-gene code communicates to the internal, then to the external. A work and role of the Holy Spirit is to preserve our going out and our coming in *{Psalms 121:7-8}*.

The blood and the heart are two main functions of the human body that everyone can physically relate to. Doctors daily carry out heart surgeries, transplants and blood transfusions in the hospital. However, the blood and heart are symbolically contrasted under the spiritual scope as matters pertaining to the spirit, the soul and the mind reflecting the activity in the heart although it's a muscle organ. The blood, the spirit, the mind and heart are one spiritually; life and substance. Oh, the Blood removes verdicts. Oh, the Blood removes curses, cycles and all that holds us bound in mind, soul and body. The Blood paid my sin debt, my death debt, incarceration debt, iniquity debt and transgression debt. The Blood liberates our reasoning, our imagination, our emotions, our desires and our will and reconciles us in the designated place as being friends of GOD. Oh, the Blood of Yeshua stands as a fortress, a fortified place, overshadowing our souls and our spirits like a canopy. *The Word of GOD declares in Psalm 91:12 He that dwells in the secret place of the Most High shall abide under the shadow of the Almighty. I will say of the LORD, He is my refuge and my fortress; my God; in Him will I trust.* This declaration can be applied by hearts that are in covenant bond with GOD. Yeshua is the Body of Christ pavilion for all who seeks Him for shelter and protection; raise the banner. Yeshua is the blood stained banner lifted **Already** in glorious victory against His enemies who are now our enemies.

Any abnormal spiritual bloodline condition or soul battle is just right for King Jesus' Victory Plan of Redemption! **It's not Religious! It's Supernatural!** Remember, bowing your heart to the call of deliverance rescues souls from chains of spiritual bondage. This is the perfect will of GOD the Father. Your True identity and inheritance is in the bloodline of Christ Jesus! He holds the Ekklesia's manifested present-future hope. Whatever has been announced or spoken toward you, about you, announced to you or presented to you that don't align with the Word of GOD is a lie from the pit of hell. **Don't Receive It! Don't Entertain It! Don't Meditate On it! And Don't Act On That Lie!** All that oppose the perfect plan of Yahweh is from the dark side. See sin as a drug addiction or a deadly virus waiting to seduce, tempt, overtake and molest our thinking, cloud our vision, character and steal our innocence. Now, see the Blood of Yeshua HaMashiach decontaminating and canceling out all the poison in our blood.

Song: Nothing, But the Blood of Jesus

(Robert Lowry)

1. What Can wash away my sins? Nothing but the Blood of Jesus;
2. For My Pardon this I See_ Nothing but the Blood of Jesus;
3. Nothing Can for the Sin Atone_ Nothing but the blood of Jesus;
4. This Is All My Hope and Peace_ Nothing but the Blood of Jesus;

What can make Me Whole Again?
Nothing but the Blood of Jesus.

For My Cleansing this I Plea
Nothing but the Blood of Jesus.

Naught of good I have been
Nothing but the Blood of Jesus.

This Is All My Righteousness
Nothing but the Blood of Jesus.

Oh, Precious Is the Flow that makes me White as Snow;

No Other Fount I Know, Nothing but The Blood of Jesus.

Spiritually speaking from what is called as the gene passing or genetic line of the seed after the fall through Satan's lie can be viewed as being the indoctrination of the imagination, the heart and the spirit of the mind. After Eve and Adam had been seduced and intoxicated by falsehood; this was the act of admission that allowed the intruder of the soul to sperm his seed. If the heart and mind are trapped and blinded this gives lead way to dysfunctional behavior. Satan needed a womb; even the darkness recognizes divine order, laws and instructions. The demonic seed generated the downward spiral of depraved mindsets. Those that live in the realm of the flesh-mind are hostile toward GOD *{Romans 8:7-8}*, but there is no law against love. The body of Yeshua, JESUS our Messiah, abolished in his flesh the hate, hostility and tore the middle partition of separation by way of the Bloody Cross to render us qualified to be brought near to GOD the Father for the remission of sin and to plead every case *{Ephesians 2:11-16}*. ABBA Father *(Greek term pater of a people)* refers to Yahweh as our father who the care giver, nourisher, upholder and protector. Yeshua has declared the souls hidden in Him to **"Be Free! Be Healed! Be Liberated!** In the Spirit of your mind, body and soul! Yeshua has declared it done **Already** through the **Power of the Finished Work of the Cross! By His Blood! By His Spirit and Water! And By His Name!** Meditate on the Word, Digest the Word and Become **One** with the Spirit of Christ! Follow ABBA's instructions and live. The plan that He has for your life will rock your world and blow your mind. *The Word of GOD declares in John 8:36 So if the Son sets you free, you will be free indeed.*

Prayer

By The AUTHORITY And POWER Of HOLY SPIRIT IN The NAME Of JESUS WE SEND And COMMAND EVERY FIERY ARROW THAT SATAN HAS THROWN TOWARD MY IDENTITY, COVENANT WITH THE LORD, MY PERSONHOOD, JOBS, FINANCES, MINISTRY, HEALTH, FAMILY, RELATIONSHIPS, MIND AND EVERY PIERCING DART OF WORDS THAT THE DEVIL HAVE SPOKEN THROUGH SOMEONE IN THE CHURCH OR IN THE WORLD TO FALL TO THE GROUND AND DIE BY THE AUTHORITY AND POWER OF THE HOLY SPIRIT! WE COMMAND IT TO BE SENT BACK TO THE SENDER IN THE NAME OF JESUS CHRIST!

Amen.

The Spirit, just as the blood, is life-forming and flows like a river to the depths of our being functioning by the design intent system of the Creator. Another task of the Ruach Hakodesh is to promote the Rivers of Living Water to flow in those that believe in Christ. The Spirit of Elohim, the Breath -Wind- is to be honored, cherished, appreciated and not taken lightly. As we look at the blood which is tangible, touchable and depended upon by mankind to survive, this liquid symbolically testifies of the supernatural importance of the Spirit of GOD living in the soul. Together as **ONE** unit the blood and the Spirit is the lifeline of the complete function of man's new nature existence. This revelation relates to the new creature that is restored through the Blood of Yeshua and the Spirit that provides continual divine restoration from day to day. *The Word of GOD declares in Leviticus 17:11 Life is in the blood.* All that pertain to the living is related and found in the blood. The blood gives life and the nature of life is in the blood itself. This is the natural order as it functions inwardly by its ordained purpose. Notice that blood needs no other help to tell it how to perform its purpose. Therefore the worth, value, authority and power is in the nature that is contained in the blood. That nature defines and reveals the very life in spirit-form as none other than our Creator, Elohim, not man nor any other false deity. Our worth, identity, being and value are in the womb of the Ruach of GOD; birthed out of the Spirit and Blood in covenant union with the true living GOD in Christ.

Transgression, iniquity, sickness, disease and all that pertained to the darkness was in the midst in the garden in the form of the forbidden fruit transferred and passed to the bloodline; affecting the blood, the line, contaminating the thought and will of man's spirit to live and walk in the full glory and dominion that was ordained by the Creator from the beginning. Satan stole Adam's *(Eve)* life, body and produced in him a dark spirit. Man's nature was reduced to being void of true Light and a stranger and enemy to the True Light. That fallen nature also was an enemy to the Presence of GOD and they became foreign to the open heaven atmosphere and to the fellowship and intimacy of worship with Yahweh-Elohim. The human life taken by another human in the Old Testament was treated with capital punishment by being stoned to death. In *{Genesis 9:6}* the punishment for that offense was death. The person that committed the crime life was to be taken. Yahweh the Father takes wickedness, rebellion and slavery to sin's power and its dominion intensely to the execution level that demands **a life for a life**. *The Word of GOD*

declares in Romans 6:22 The wages of sin is death, but the gift of Yahweh is everlasting life. Sin's wages bring on death; death brings on separation, alienation from GOD spiritually and then physically before taking its grip for complete condemnation if ones heart does not truly repent. How does this affect us as Christians since we are saved? When sin is conceived and concealed, its code is to hinder and do harm spiritually and mentally. Sin that is not addressed through a change of mind as to casting it off as a filthy stained garment or laying every leading weight aside through washing of the WORD in the heart, in word and in deed will form a hiding place in that heart. Consider a sore that never heals; it is painful when touched, tender to the touch, aggravated, sensitive and expands deeper and doesn't heal properly due to other repetitious aggravation. Sins that are attached through a stronghold in the mindset can hide and rise with the same symptoms as this sore. The open wounded sore in the heart will make the heart become callous and cancerous to the whole body and possibly affecting others that come into contact directly or indirectly. These sins that seem small can spread like gangrene destroying whatever and whoever gets it its way. The heart being a very pliable muscle is the reflector of inner feelings, emotions, thoughts, the human will and temperament. And when these emotions are stirred to action, the sin or evil that may have been planted first in thought now become a reality of negative energy that plays its darkness out through that wounded soul and body. A majority of the time a person does not see or recognize the unseen demonic force that has planned a downfall. Episodes at any degree is overcome by application of the **Word of GOD** continually to the mind and heart personally becoming **ONE**; deleting mixture, renouncing the voice and power of darkness and honoring the blood. The power of the blood is invoked and honored in the heavenly realm from a heart that is genuine and trusting in the power of the finished work of the Cross. **Deliverance is the Children's Bread!** We often look at the bigger sins or the ones many call big, if that's the case, lets add these to that list that targets souls for spiritual imprisonment and bondage. Remember, Satan has no new tricks and no new games only new faces that aren't familiar with his plots of deception or souls that reject the knowledge and wisdom of Christ. The objective of this study manual is to expose the work of darkness, sin and to spiritually jump start the DNA GOD-gene in you! The heart relates to the spiritual. The mind relates to the spiritual. And the soul relates to the spiritual. We are spiritual beings in a body. Unclean spirits work through minds that have opened themselves up to the devil through open gates. All desires are not evident, mostly the actions from the dark hidden desire. And these gates are not always recognized, but some of the gates are called eye gate, ear gate, hand, mouth and nose gate, as well as, your body; all instruments. We are commanded to put off the mind of the flesh and its deeds and to put on Christ. Do not allow another mind -thought- outside of the thought of GOD create anything within your universe. The universe called the spirit of your mind, heart, soul and body. You have a new wind, a new mind, a new heart, a new tongue, a new nature, a new soul, a new name, a new position and a new walk.

- *The Word of GOD declares in Romans 6:13 Do not offer any part of yourself to sin as an instrument of wickedness, but rather offer yourselves to God as those who have been brought from death to life; and offer every part of yourself to him as an instrument of righteousness.*

Light will always reflect light and darkness will always reflect darkness. There is no one righteous or perfect outside of CHRIST

JESUS! The Church, believers, righteousness and perfection and identity are found to be complete in Him alone. Therefore, being In HIM makes believers righteous and perfect; IN CHRIST. GOD commands the Church, not the world, to love Him with ALL of our heart, our entire mind and soul which reflects His character. The Church, each believer, must examine self by **the Word! By the Word, the WORD** making certain none of these intruding unclean spirit- minds have lodged in the universe of the mind and soul and heart. The image in the mirror must reflect the image of Yahweh. The term image derives from the *Hebrew* word *tselem* meaning a representation, a manifestation of the original and a shadow of things to come.

When we know what the intruder looks like, then we can better protect, dress and arm ourselves spiritually. Below are prototypes *(first of its kind)* that can manifest themselves if the heart is not guarded by the Spirit of Holiness and not grounded in Truth. The intruder will attempt through any outlet or foot hold to come in for the purpose of claiming territory and setting up his camp. **The Blood of Yeshua Never Loses Its Power!** It triumphs over every serpent or python spirit. *The Word of GOD declares in Luke 10:19 Behold, I give unto you power to tread on serpents and scorpions and over all the power of the enemy and nothing shall by any means hurt you.* Remember, it's supernatural. *The Word of GOD declares in Psalms 107:20 He sent His Word and healed them (us), and delivered from their destructions.* Receive it in every area and stand in the gap for others.

**In order to pray and decree heaven's access, you must be born again of the Spirit of Christ *{John 3:1-21; Romans 6;23; 10:9}*... pray sincerely the prayer below to receive eternal salvation. I pray that you are lead of Holy Spirit to be planted in a Word-Faith Base Church and baptised that you may be nourished and developed spiritually for advancement in the Kingdom of GOD in this life.

Christ Is the Door:

Heavenly Father (Yahweh), In the Name of (Yeshua) Jesus, I Repent of All My Sins. I Ask That You Forgive Me, Cleanse Me, Wash Me With Your Blood And Word? I Ask That You Come Into My Heart To Be My Savior And My Lord? I Freely Give You Access To The Throne Of My Heart. Your Word Tells Me, That The Wages of Sin is death, But The Gift Of GOD Is Eternal Life. Your Word Tells Me, If I Confess With My Mouth And Believe In My Heart That GOD Raised Jesus from The Dead, I Shall Be Saved. I Confess Unto Salvation And I Believe In My Heart Unto Righteousness That I Am Justified... By Faith I Receive Your Grace Provision, Heavenly Father, Fill Me with Your Holy Spirit In Jesus Name.

Amen.

Bloodline Prayer:

In the Name of Jesus Christ, I Praise You Lord and Honor the Blood In Every Area of My Life. I Repent And Remove All Restrictions In (Yeshua) Jesus Name. I Implore Your Cleansing And the Sanctifying Work Of Holy Spirit To Cleanse My Bloodline from this Generation Back. I Ask You LORD Whatever Is In My Bloodline That Opposes the Image of GOD, Remove It Father In Yeshua's Name. By the Authority and Power Of Holy Spirit I Bind And Break the Chain of Every Smoking demon, Alcohol demon, Lazy demon, Jezebel demon, Ahab demon, Lukewarm demon, Ego demon, Self-pity demon, School dropout demon, Poverty Mindset demon, Rejection, Mean-spirited, Control demon and Deep Hurt demon, Be Broken Off My Bloodline In Jesus Name. I Lift Up My Seed And My Seed Seed to You Father; Sever Every Unclean Spirit That Appears In the Bloodline to Alter Their (our, my) Relationship, Health, Purpose, Vision, Destiny and Walk With You Lord In the Name of Jesus Christ. I Pray for the Release of Your Bloodline Riches To Be Poured Into Our (my) Mind, Our Thought, Imagination and Action. I Plead the Blood Against Every Hereditary Disease, Sickness, Barrenness or Abnormality That Attempts To Show Up In My Bloodline In the Name Of Jesus Christ. I Plead the Blood Against Every Deficiency That Causes My Children or Grandchildren Not to Excel. I Plead the Blood of Yeshua Against Every Abomination Thought And I Speak Death To Seeds of Identity Confusion In

Jesus Name. I Loose the Healing Virtue to Flow Through the Brain Cells, Heart Valves, Ovaries, Testicles, Breast Cells, Nerves, Organs, Veins, Muscles and the Nervous System In the Name Of Yeshua. I Command the (my) Body to Awaken And Respond Daily To the WORD of Life And Healing In Jesus Name.

Amen.

Every Power Be Broken By The Blood Of Yeshua HaMashiach (Jesus Christ).

• Spirit of Sabotage
• Spirit of Blockage
• Spirit of Competiveness
• Spirit of Greed
• Spirit of Slumber
• Spirit of Lasciviousness
• Spirit of Covetousness
• Spirit of Outrage
• Spirit of Bitterness
• Spirit of Struggle
• Spirit of Porn
• Spirit of Racism
• Spirit of Retaliation
• Spirit of Heaviness
• Spirit of Unforgiving
• Spirit of Fear
• Spirit of Phobia
• Spirit of Paranoia
• Spirit of Depression
• Spirit of Revenge
• Spirit of Pride
• Spirit of Lack
• Spirit of Divination
• Spirit of Domination
• Spirit of Deep hurt
• Spirit of Rejection
• Spirit of Jealousy
• Spirit of Double-mindedness
• Spirit of Whoredom
• Spirit of Gambling
• Spirit of Spite
• Spirit of Malice
• Spirit of Confusion
• Spirit of Gloom
• Spirit of Callus
• Spirit of Conspiracy
• Spirit of Vagabond
• Spirit of Hatred
• Spirit of Low Self-Esteem
• Spirit of Doubt
• Spirit of Rebellion
• Spirit of Controlling

Faith Affirmation:

Thank You LORD, As A Son of GOD, I Am Whole Mind, Spirit, Soul And Body. As A Son I Am Walking By FAITH In The Manifested Power and Ability That You Have Given To Me From This Day Forward, No Turning Back! Nothingness, I Am Free! Because I Am A Son of GOD. I Talk Whole, I See Whole, I Think Whole, I Live Whole, I Love Whole And My Body Is Whole! I Decree That Every Door of Prosperity and Health Be Accelerated In My New Life Hidden In Christ! As A Son of GOD I Give Access To The WORD And Apply the WORD of GOD To Every Place In My Mind!

Amen.

Write Out Your Bloodline Prayer To Pray:

The Eternal Word is the mirror to our souls and the answer to any issue of the bloodline and abnormalities of the heart; mild or great, light or heavy. All heart defects of the mind and soul call for the washing of the Word through the Blood of Jesus by the Spirit and a bowing down, releasing one's own pattern of thinking! These demonic intruders have been nailed to the Cross. And because it's nailed to the Cross sons and daughters of Yahweh are not to take part of what is dead. When the serpent appears crush him with the Word of Truth. Jesus releases access to heal any open wound, break fetters that lock the mind with false impressions, illusions, tie up demonic activity, close the door on yokes that bind and cause harm to self, others, alienation and spiritual death. Desires are what ideals and thoughts build on. **True Authority** and **Power** is only accessed to hearts and souls through commitment and seeking Yahweh's deliverance through His Son Yeshua HaMashiach. Access is already granted by the Father through Holy Spirit to the worshiper who trades his stained garment for the garment of righteousness. *The Word of GOD declares in 2 Corinthians 10:5 We demolish arguments and every pretension that sets itself up against the knowledge of God, and we take captive every thought to make it obedient to Christ.*

The scriptures reveals that the blood of slain unblemished bulls and sheep that were sacrificed were looked upon symbolically as being holy *(set apart)*, a point of contact that was sanctioned by GOD for the Priest to sanctify and make atonement *(cover)* for the sins of the nation. This was done on the altar and upon entering into the Holy of Holies once a year to offer blood on the mercy seat in the Holy Presence of Yahweh; from the people to the Priest *(also his household)* to Yahweh and from Yahweh to the Priest to the people on the Day of Atonement *{Leviticus 16:15}.* This holy point of contact in that dispensation gave the erring, adulterous people the right, the access and grace to be cleansed, sanctified, rescued and brought into right standing and right fellowship with GOD through their surrendering and willingness to heed instructions and obey. Their obedience released covenant promises, favor, removed His wrath and turned curses away from them through repentance. Blessings reign, rule and have dominion through submission and obedient faithful and repentant hearts. The Peace of Yeshua places worshipers under the canopy of amazing sacrificial love, favor, protection, promise and called believers His covenant people. The animal sacrifice was symbolic of covenant agreement, covering, a substitute for their life and an example of what should be done to unrepentant rebellious souls. The life of the soul making the offering was identified with the life of the sacrificial animal offering being made for the atonement. No blood was to be consumed by anyone at anytime nor in any dispensation, even in this dispensation of grace which we are living in; the Age of Grace *{Leviticus 17:10}*. All the sacrificial feasts of the LORD pointed to the Lamb of Yahweh. Yeshua was offered up as the scapegoat, the Azazel who took away the sins; the ultimate living sacrifice for the sins of the human family and the spiritual deformity of a dark world. The blood that carries our God-gene identity is like a blood transfusion that transfers the divine nature's wealth: dominion, character, mind, thought, attitude, inheritance and birthright, etc. The Spirit of GOD sealed the work of the Cross. When the Spirit of Christ enters into the human spirit of a soul to be LORD *(reign and rule with all authority and all power)* all that doesn't belong to you as a son or daughter will be terminated from the new building *(spirit, soul, body)* for the renovation by the new land owner, King Jesus. Yahweh in Christ gives believers the right to act, the right of authority and access only through the precious blood of His Lamb, His Word and His Spirit; the DNA of the Kingdom of GOD in Christ.

Hebrew terms for Repentance
Teshuvah: change of mind, to change the way of thinking
(resulting in change that is revealed in character)

The Lord's strategies and victory shown through believers bring confusion to the camp of the enemy. Taking the fight in spiritual warfare with supernatural spiritual weapons is a Kingdom benefit. Spiritual things cannot be fixed by natural means. Shift from that carnal image of action and reverse that desire that seeks to manipulate your being that isn't of the realm of light and life. GOD is bigger, greater than any disease, any threat, any disappointment, any lose and any pain. It has no jurisdiction over Him or those that belong to Him. When one realizes their birthright and that the Ruach Hakodesh *(GOD Holy Spirit)* lives within that give a soul the power to war back. Holy Spirit lives in the true believer with designed purpose, waiting to rise up and to fill you continuously with His divine power of demonstration. "GREATER LIVES IN YOU!" The Spirit of Christ raises you up and brings you out with His high hand of victory. That's the territory of victory and testimony we proclaim in the LORD! That's how we conquer the schemes, sin, wrong persuasion, ungodly cycles, wrong motives and establish new beginnings through the course of our resurrected new life. Don't entertain something that has been around longer than flesh; flesh has no power to win if you rule well by the Ruach Hakodesh *(Holy Spirit)*. **"I Decree That You Govern-Rule Well."**

At the end of chapter 1 illustration A which shows Adam's *(Eve)* spiritual state in Eden before the falling away. Illustrations B and C will show you an example of the soul without Christ, the compromising or backslidden soul and the soul with Christ. The demonstration is to show you a visual illustrational idea of what the man in the mirror looks like spiritually under the supernatural divine scope of Yahweh, the Father. The diagram illustrated below gives a view of a heart when sin is actively lodged in the soul and how it effects the total being of a person; spirit, mind, soul and body. When there is Light in the human spirit it will shine forth like a lantern illuminating the heart and releasing the power source to master sin instead of the sin mastering the soul. Growing and maturing is both the natural and the spiritual process. However, don't let sin reign and overtake you by playing on the enemy's ground or falling prey to his sway. He plays to keep and to destroy that which he keeps. It is a cost for anyone to remain in ignorance! *The Word of GOD declares in Hebrew 11:25b There is pleasure in sin for a season.* Anybody can get hooked thinking I can stop when I am ready. That's what the deceiver wants many to think. It's growth when a soul can see than I *(self)* need to be dethroned. It takes a made up mind and will with the help of Holy Spirit to straighten crooked paths. Sin is sin in the court of Yahweh. Whatsoever it maybe our prayers should be *"SEARCH ME LORD, MAKE THE CROOKED PATH STRAIGHT, RENEW A RIGHT SPIRIT WITHIN ME AND CLEANSE THE DEEPNESS OF MY HEART SO I WILL BE A SANCTUARY FOR YOU TO DWELL IN. I WANT TO BE RIGHT WITH YOU LORD!"* The will of a soul must come subject to the will of the WORD.

Illustration B shows the example of the universe of the soul without light in a naked, compromised or backslidden condition. The arrows show the activity of sins location and how it rules the fleshly inclinations in the mind and heart through free will through the body. In a few pages illustration C shows the soul in its new condition, having Christ in the center of ones life and heart to dismantle all forces and distortion in the soul and behavior in the present state; establishing the identity of the DNA Seed of Righteousness. **Holy Spirit work brings TRANSFORMATION from the inside out!** See it for what it is bondage and spiritual bleeding. We are healed through the act of acknowledging it, repenting and forgiving. Be set free in the spirit of your mind! *(outer circle- body; inner circle- soulish realm; center circle- spirit).*

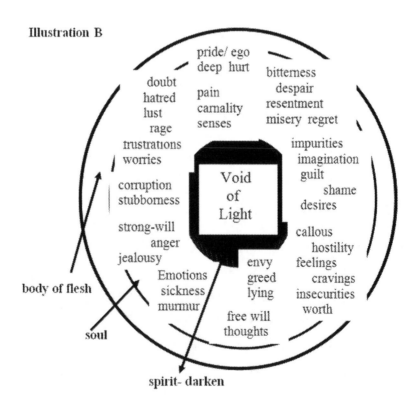

- *The Word of GOD declares in 1 Chronicles 7:14 If my people who are called by My Name will humble themselves, pray and seek my face and turn from there wicked ways, then Jehovah will hear from heaven and Jehovah will forgive their sin and will heal their land.*

- *The Word of GOD declares in 1 Samuel 15:22 Obedience is far better than sacrifice.*

- *The Word of GOD declares in Proverbs 4:23 Keep your heart with all diligences; for out of it are the issues of life.*

GOD has the power to release blessings according to our choice-paths we decide to take. Yahweh *(Jehovah)* provision is for His chosen is to choose life and blessings, so that we may live and our seed may live the abundant life hidden in Christ Jesus as they walk in the statutes of the LORD. As we are in Christ, His love covers a multitude of offenses in which we have repented of by washing our slate white as snow. Blemishes that aren't seen in the illustration below shows how the blood washes our conditions and the work of Holy Spirit continues to fill us bringing wholeness, health and empowerment to accomplish great things in the site of the LORD. This is how the Father sees a believer through the Blood of Jesus when sin is denounced, forgiven and not practiced, washed and purged. *(outer circle- body; inner circle- soulish realm; center circle- spirit).*

Illustration C

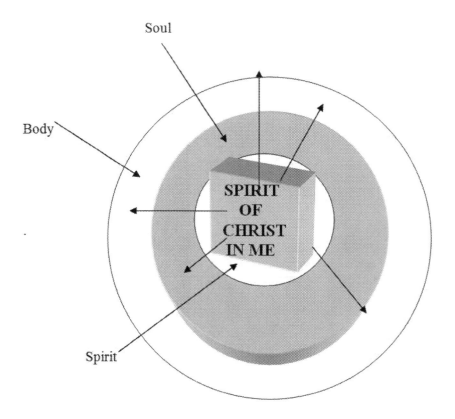

The Redemption Plan inaugurated to redeem and deliver mankind through blood sacrifice from condemnation, impurities and the rupture of its fabric inwardly reinstating us back into the Royal Family of Jehovah *(Yahweh)* and Yeshua. We are His creation and the workmanship of His hand through the working of Ruach Hakodesh *(Holy Spirit)*. The Church has been purchased with the price of a royal life and royal blood. Yeshua, the Passover Lamb of GOD is the substitute for the sinner, breaking every curse released through the fall and positioning believers as sons. Yeshua took our place on the Cross of death to bring reconciliation and the peace of GOD to humanity *{John 3:16-21}*. He became the curse and took the curse in His flesh in order to remove the curse that we deserved. Yeshua told all his disciples to do this in remembrance of me, take, eat this is my body broken for you; and take, drink this is my blood shed for you *{John 6:54-54}*. He is the Covenant that restores dominion, authority and opens the spiritual womb that souls are united in covenant. The flesh does not avail, but the supernatural power of the DNA of the Blood of Christ avails on the mercy seat for our hang ups, character flaws and offenses of the heart, soul and body. The Spirit of Christ is the life giving Spirit that breathes life and resuscitates. Tell the devil, "I'm free and I am taking what belongs to me back in Yeshua's name." Tell the devil, "GET BACK!" THE LORD REBUKES YOU! I have a new identity, a new divine nature and my name is written in the book of life and the WORD is stamped on the tablet of my heart. I'm purchased with the Supernatural DNA of the Blood of YESHUA. My divine identity is in the blood and my identity is released for expression in every area of my hidden life in Christ for the display of God's Glory through Holy Spirit. This womb is not yours, it's the Lord's. We can only make these affirmations effectively when the heart has genuinely been reborn and submerged in the Spirit and baptized in the Fire of GOD.

Praise the Lord Jesus Christ for the place and rank that He has positioned His tribe through His blood and His Spirit. The Lion and Tribe of Judah present our new reflection and our new position in Christ. In times of testing, seasons of change, tribulation and trials we are to encourage ourselves and declare to the heavens from a legal stance. As you look at each identity phrase they decree your **Oneness** with the Promise. Divine power is unlocked through the keys of divine wisdom and the knowledge of divine Truth *(chapter 5)*. When we are one in Christ the spiritual womb, fabric and union are knitted together in the mind, spirit, soul and body. Remember, the covenant union is a holy **marriage**; the Church *(Bride of Christ)* and Christ *(Head of the Church-Believer)*. Study, mediate and memorize scriptural verses that support your identity *(few pages ahead)* by writing them on the table of your heart and the frontlet of your mind daily. The Word is Spirit, Holy and Supernatural! When the **Word** *(essence of ABBA)* which is seed is scattered in good soil, the soul and heart, will reap the spiritual and physical benefits of the divine nature. *The Word of GOD declares in Revelation 1:18 Yeshua (Jesus) said, I AM the First and the Last, the Living One. I was dead and behold, now I AM alive forever and ever. And I hold the keys of Death and of Hades.* What can wash away my sins, my guilt, shame and my past and restore and pardon me? Nothing but the Blood of JESUS! The Spirit of Christ DNA Makes Us Whole Again! And His Righteousness Transforms Us and His Spirit Conforms Us to His likeness! The Blood of Yeshua HaMashiach satisfies the Justice Courts of the Kingdom of Yahweh. In His death and resurrection Yeshua retrieved the keys stolen from Adam and have released them to the Body of Christ.

- *The Word of GOD declares in 1 John 3:8-10a {ESV} The reason the Son of GOD appeared was to destroy the works of the evil one. No one born of GOD makes a practice of sinning, for God's Seed abides in him, he cannot keep on sinning, because he has been born of GOD. By this it is evident who are the children of GOD, and who are the children of the devil: whoever does not practice righteousness is not of GOD, nor is the one who does not love his brother-sister.*

Man is a trichotomy with a spirit and a soul clothed in a bodysuit of flesh. The Apostle Paul confirms in the scripture *{2 Thessalonians 5:23}* that man is a tri-part being; spirit, soul and body and all three must be kept blameless in the Lord. The soulish realm is composed of the will, desires, emotions, feelings, imaginations, reasoning, ego and conscience. It also includes the senses that allow touching, tasting, seeing smelling and hearing. Just as the human body has a physical anatomy, the **Ruach of Yahweh** *(Spirit of Yahweh)* also has a supernatural anatomy. The Spirit of Yahweh Elohim takes on many manifestations. The Ruach of GOD anatomy is able to hear, act, speak, breathe, expose, reveal, overshadow, has emotions, smells, sees, touches and intervenes with the cosmic, mankind and nature. Elohim's power has the ability within itself to become substance. Now faith is the substance of things hoped for the evidence of things not seen *{Hebrews 11:1}*.

The devil appeared with the sons of GOD *(the angels)* in scripture. He, the counterfeiter, hears and falsifies what he hears. The devil's gene seeks to pervert all that is good and all that belongs to the family of GOD in Yeshua HaMashiach *(Christ Jesus)*. When Elohim gave Adam the law concerning their wealth inheritance maintenance in Eden, Satan also heard the announcement of the ruling. Satan used what was said in the atmospheric realm against Adam and Eve. This strategy is happening today. When ABBA releases through the Ruach divine gifts, anointing, blessings, favor, instructions, revelation of the Word and direction the devil is right there to challenge your worth, your character, your thought, to set up deterrence, your ability to create and to weaken your faith. But the Word of GOD never fails as we stand our ground in the faith.

We understand the first Adam became a living being, created by Yahweh Elohim from red dust of the ground, made in the image of YHWH and the head of human race. We understand that Yeshua HaMashiach *(Jesus Christ)* is the last ADAM *(not a second Adam)* the Life-Giving Spirit head of the spiritual redeemed race *{1 Corinthians 15:22, 45}.* Before anything existed it was **Already** in the thought and purpose of Elohim. The natural sphere is seen as the photocopy of the unseen spiritual realm, not the other way around. Therefore, things which we may see or hear take place in the unseen spirit world first. The good has characteristic traits and the evil has characteristic traits. Character and spirit can be viewed parallel due to the common source which is the nature within that represents what it is. For an example peas beget peas and berries beget berries. If the tree bared mixed fruit there will be a mixture not a true fruit. *The Word of GOD declares in James 1:8 A double minded man is unstable in all his ways.* Why? There is a mixture and there would be two thoughts or two minds. Remember, the DNA seed imprints its own character traits and substance. They bear consequences upon the soul that fellowships, partners or partake of its fruit creating a covenant. Whatever is done in the kingdom of darkness or the Kingdom of Light will reflect on or in the physical sphere through the spirit or character of a soul. Therefore, the **SPIRIT-FILLED** Church with **One** mind, **One** thought, carries the keys and whole judicial responsibility in the realm of the spirit to wage war against all forms of sin, evil and wickedness, to denounce it and to proclaim the promised favor of GOD in that season. **"I DECREE YOU WILL WALK IN THE SINGLE HEARTED-MIND OF CHRIST AND CREATE HIS BUSINESS!"** Everything that wants to cling in double mindedness is broken off of you now in the Name of JESUS- Yeshua HaMashiach. **"I Decree Double Blessings Overtake Your Being in the Powerful**

Name of Yeshua." The **WORD of GOD** is the **SWORD of the SPIRIT**; wave your Sword righteously in the realm of the spirit.

Believers are the light of the world, the light on our jobs, in our families and in the market place. It is a part of our DNA to bring order where there is chaos or confusion by the leading wisdom of the Ruach of Elohim. Our new realm of thinking, under the influence of the mind of Christ, elevates us above the realm of darkness and teaches us how to use our power and revelatory gifts in this world. That means we not only operate from a higher dimension, but the favor obtained from walking in the new life releases the answers and solutions to issues pertaining to life; ours and others. The Church who's Head is Christ has the divine answer to meet the needs of a people. And the Law of the Kingdom provides the love for the guidance of the Body of Christ. It is not wise to leave the HEAD -Christ- and override the RUACH. Eve demonstrated the situation that we can learn from in Eden. The Glory is released only in Christ to His Bride, not outside of Christ, ABBA will not share His Glory with any graven image!

The DNA is the molecule of new life. Just as blood is the lifeline of oxygen for the human body organ the Holy Spirit functions as the oxygen source for the new life of believers in Christ. The Ruach Hakodesh is the molecule of life that transmits from the King's throne what is on His heart for His sons and daughters. The Holy Spirit distributes all the new to the new building. He supplies what is needed in the temple. He exposes, disposes and cleanses blemishes out of the temple; keeping the temple holy, bring holy conviction when sin, compromise is present so the believing soul can make a sober choice to comply with the heavenly rule. The divine Molecule of Life gives strength to the heart and mind during times of weakness, hardship and suffering. He teaches, guides, instructs, builds, comforts, rebukes, corrects, admonishes, fills, dwells and speaks beyond the cosmos into the thoughts and hearts chamber of man's soul igniting a light in forms of a fire, wind or even a small still voice. When the **Fire** is ignited in your hearts and souls and mind you must allow the **Fire of GOD** to penetrate through constant intimacy which brings His *Shekinah* Glory. Ruach is the Fire- power that delivers and cast out demons! The Fire that baptizes and the Fire that consumes darkness! It is He who answers by fire! The Fire that burns up all that the enemy places before you! The Fire that promotes and elevates! The Fire that scatters your enemy and the Fire that fills your spirit, empowers you and sanctifies you! He is the Fire that leads you when things appear to be dark! Ruach Hakodesh is the Fire that heals, protects, purges, exalts and comforts you! He is the Fire! We are conforming, transforming and changing into the likeness of our elder brother, Yeshua by the power of the Fire of GOD.

The Presence of GOD is needed in this atmosphere bringing transformation, purifying and bringing knowledge that is the life substance for the worshiper. The DNA *(divine nature)* Molecule of Life that operates behind the scenes in the unseen realm and tabernacles in the hearts of saints governs in overpowering the darkness and infirmities of the soul bringing divine blessings of manifestation. He prays through the believers the will and utterances of ABBA. Even when hopelessness attempts to invade our atmosphere the DNA molecule of the Ruach is our present help. The Spirit of Christ makes intercession for the church continuously; for that reason, the Church must be willing partakers in seeking and crying out to ABBA. In Yahweh's appointed time, Ruach Hakodesh *(Holy Spirit)* is always there to take back what was stolen or given away in ignorance to the devil. At no time will the Ruach Hakodesh leave or forsake us. When we lift up our eyes from that place of dryness, distress, anguish, unproductiveness, loneliness or despair the divine molecule of life will speak forth a word into the believer's spirit that will transform your moment and heart in that season for life. The Ruach confirms and assures to the believer the will of ABBA. Ruach declares there is no failure in The LORD! Ruach declares there is no defeat in The LORD! The Ruach of the LORD declares there is no shadow of turning in the LORD and that which the LORD has promised concerning you is declared to come to pass by His hand for His name sake. Your status is to remain in faith and obedience watered in love. ***The Word of GOD declares in 1 Corinthians 15:58 Be ye steadfast, unmovable, always abounding in the work of the Lord, forasmuch as ye know that your labor is not in vain in the Lord.*** Yahweh is not a man that He shall lie, nor the son of man that he shall repent *{Numbers 23:19}.* If the LORD has spoken it *(salvation for your seed, divine deliverance, healing, promotion, peace, joy, dominion, power, divine knowledge, virtue, wisdom, provision, anointing, elevation, restoration, retribution, increase, double anointing for the trouble, divine revelation),* the promise shall come to pass by faith. The divine molecule of life *(Holy Spirit)* has everything you need pertaining to life and godliness. It was established for the children of Yahweh before the foundation of the world and for the Body of Christ to have dominion in the earth realm. Yahweh authorized it! It is the faith-logical Presence-sphere. It takes faith to get you there and it takes faith to elevate you to the next dimension of faith and the next and the next and the next. Faith levels elevates beyond saving faith. The power substance is dimensionally. It creates and takes the sons of GOD to higher dimensions in GOD. It is the will of the Yahweh in Yeshua.

MY IDENTITY IN YESHUA HAMASHIACH

- **I AM CREATED IN THE IMAGE OF GOD!**

Genesis 1:27

- **I AM REDEEMED!**

Galatians 3:13-14

- **I AM SIGNIFICANT!**

1 Peter 2:9

- **I AM DELIVERED!**

Colossians 1:13

- **I AM A PARTAKER WITH CHRIST!**

Hebrew 3:14

- **I AM DEAD TO SIN AND ALIVE IN CHRIST!**

Romans 6:11

- **I AM SEATED IN HEAVENLY PLACES WITH CHRIST JESUS!**

Ephesians 2:6

- **I AM THE WORKMANSHIP OF YAHWEH!**

Ephesians 2:10

- **I AM CONVINCED THAT ALL THINGS WORK TOGETHER FOR MY GOOD!**

Romans 8:28

- **I AM COURAGEOUS, FULL OF POWER, LOVE & A SOUND MIND!**

Timothy 1:17

- **I AM A BRANCH OF THE TRUE VINE!**

John 15:1-5

- **I AM THE SALT OF THE EARTH!**

Matthew 5:13

- **I AM LIGHT TO THE WORLD!**

Matthew 5:14

- **I AM GUIDED BY THE SPIRIT!**

Galatians 5:19

- **I AM PERSEVERING!**

Philippians 3:14

- **I AM A SON OF YAHWEH IN CHRIST JESUS!**

Romans 8:14-15

- **I AM ONE WITH CHRIST JESUS!**

1 Corinthians 6:17

- **I AM RIGHTEOUS AND HOLY!**

Ephesians 4:24

- **I AM MADE PERFECT!**

John 17:21-23

- **I AM SANCTIFIED!**

1 Corinthians 1:2

- **I AM FEARFULLY AND WONDERFULLY MADE!**

Psalm 139:14

- **I AM UNIQUE!**

Psalm 119:73-74

- **I AM FORGIVEN OF ALL MY SINS!**

Colossians 1:13-14

- **I AM FREE FROM CONDEMNATION!**

Romans 8:1-2

- **I AM THE HEAD NOT THE TAIL, ABOVE NOT BENEATH!**

Deuteronomy 28:13

- **I AM APPOINTED TO BEAR FRUIT OF RIGHTEOUSNESS!**

John 15:16

- **I AM EMPOWERED TO DO ALL THINGS THROUGH CHRIST!**

Philippians 4:13

- **I AM A CITIZEN OF HEAVEN!**

Philippians 3:20

- **I AM A NEW CREATION IN CHRIST!**

2 Corinthians 5:17

- **I AM IN THE ROYAL FAMILY!**
Ephesians 2:19

- **I AM BLAMELESS!**
1 Corinthians 1:8

- **I AM A FRIEND OF GOD!**
John 15:15

- **I AM IN A WEALTHY PLACE!**
Psalm 66:12

- **I AM IN A SAFE PLACE!**
Proverbs 18:10

- **I AM EMPOWERED TO OVERCOME!**
1 John 4:4

- **I AM QUALIFIED!**
Colossians 1:13

- **I AM STRONG!**
Psalm 68:35

- **I AM IN CHRIST AND HE IS IN ME!**
1 John 4:5

- **I AM JUSTIFIED!**
Romans 5:1

- **I AM HIDDEN IN CHRIST JESUS!**
Colossians 3:3

- **I AM HEALED!**

Isaiah 53:5

- **I AM SET FREE IN CHRIST!**

Galatians 2:4

- **I AM THE TEMPLE OF THE LIVING GOD!**

1 Corinthians 3:4-6

- **I AM AN ENEMY OF THE DEVIL! HE IS MY ADVERSARY!**

1 Peter 5:8

- **I AM BLESSED WITH EVERY SPIRITUAL BLESSING!**

Ephesians 1:3

- **I AM A MINISTER OF RECONCILIATION!**

2 Cor. 5:17-21

- **I AM CREATED TO CREATE!**

Philippians 4:19

- **I AM THE RIGHTEOUSNESS OF YAHWEH IN CHRIST!**

2 Corinthians 5:21

- **I AM THE JUST LIVING BY FAITH!**

Habakkuk 2:4

- **I AM CREATED FOR PURPOSE & DESTINY!**

Jeremiah 29:11

- **I AM A MASTERPIECE BY DESIGN!**

Ephesians 2:10

- **I AM AN INTERCESSOR!**

Philippians 4:6

- **I AM PROSPEROUS!**

3 John 1:2

- **I AM PROTECTED!**

Psalm 91

- **I AM PREDESTINED TO REIGN!**

Ephesians 1:5

- **I AM VICTORIOUS!**

1 Corinthians 15:57

- **I AM MORE THAN A CONQUERER!**

Romans 8:37

- **I AM A SON OF LIGHT NOT DARKNESS!**

1Thessalonians 5:5

- **I AM A SPIRITUAL HOUSE BUILT BY SPIRITUAL HANDS!**

1 Peter 2:5

- **I AM SPIRITUAL!**

1 Corinthians 2: 9-10

- **I AM THE SHEEP OF HIS PASTURE!**

Psalm 100:3

- **I AM AN AMBASSADOR FOR CHRIST!**

2 Corinthians 5:20

- **I AM CONFIDENT THAT EVERY GOOD WORK THAT CHRIST BEGIN IN ME HE WILL COMPLETE!**

Philippians 1:6

- **I AM FULLY PERSUADED THAT NOTHING CAN SEPARATE ME FROM THE LOVE OF GOD!**

Romans 8:38

- **I AM ESTABLISHED! I AM ANOINTED! I AM SEALED!**

2 Corinthians 1:21-22

- **I AM COMPLETE IN CHRIST!**

Colossians 2:9-10

- **I AM POWERFUL AGAINST SIN, TEMPTATION & ADVERSITY!**

Ephesians 6:10-18

- **I AM A WORSHIPER!**

John 9:31

- **I AM NOT ALONE!**

Hebrews 13:5

I AM NOT MY OWN! I'VE BEEN PURCHASED BY THE BLOOD OF YESHUA HAMASHIACH, THE SEED OF RIGHTEOUSNESS. THEREFORE, I AM HEALED, TRANSFORMED, ACQUITED, EMPOWERED, AUTHORIZED, ANOINTED, APPOINTED, CALLED, CHOSEN, GIVEN A NEW NAME, A NEW POSITION AND ORDAINED! I AM MADE NEW IN YESHUA! I AM IS MY TRUE DIVINE NATURE- IDENTITY IN CHRIST JESUS!

Lord, You have created me for Your glory; You
have formed me and made me.

Isaiah 43:7

5

KINGDOM MIND

The Ruach of God's wisdom supersedes man's limited intellectual knowledge, desires, and affections. The Spirit- Mind of Christ is the Mind of the King and His Kingdom. When one has been regenerated the Spirit is reversed; bought out of the state of enslavement to sin, darkness and its owner. Now the Spirit- Mind of Christ, who is GOD, of the new building *(Spirit, soul and body)* is King. The breath and mind of GOD is one imprint. The mind is powerfully unlimited. The mind, the thought, reasoning and character must be cultivated in Christ for the purpose of responding, acting, seeing as He sees, hearing as He speaks and governing in the earth as it is in the Kingdom. Yeshua HaMashiach *(Jesus Christ)* made a weighty statement regarding the thoughts and words of Yahweh GOD in *John 12:45-50*. As you ponder these verses you will see they give a supernatural, yet physical connection with the Kingdom and its government. First, Yeshua informs us that the one who looks at Him is seeing the one who sent Him. He tells us that He came as light so that those who believe in Him should not stay in darkness. The next thing He utters is if anyone hears...For I *(Yeshua)* did not speak on my own, but the Father who sent me commanded me to say all that I have spoken; so whatever I say is just what the Father has told me to say. This is the acceleration of the gift from the Kingdom -Mind of Christ- to believing believers whose paradigm is transitioning to the next and the next and next dimensions in GOD. The Kingdom Mind is a skillful mind which is constant in elevation. It is the interlocked thought reflections of GOD, full of light and born of GOD. When the mind is acceptable to the Light exposure *(Jesus Christ)*, the Light will spread like smoke in the arena of the psyche by faith. Divine thinking linked to divine imagination linked to divine faith linked to the divine Word is like a magnetic force resulting in supernatural attractions released in the physical realm. The **Kingdom-Mind of Christ** is not the mind of this world nor does it resemble this world or the flesh. It's not the mind of human beings or culture. It doesn't think, respond, move, adjust to any situations in this atmosphere; it isn't intimidated by intellect nor is it is controlled by anyone or anything in this world. The Kingdom Mind isn't a mind that can be mastered, manipulated, governed or judged by this world, but it is the mind that releases and attracts the power to overcome and rule. It is the supernatural mind imprint that connects the believer to GOD and His Kingdom. The Kingdom Mind is from GOD, of GOD and is God's heart, character and Spirit. The Kingdom Mind is relatively an enormous capacity of spiritual blessings that are in the genetic marrow of the Seed of Righteousness ready to be submerged for the activation through of the inner parts of the new creature. The Kingdom Mind is the heart of GOD performing through hungry, thirsty and humbling hearts. The Kingdom Mind communicates God's judgments in thoughts reflecting divine order, righteousness, creativity, honesty, love, loyalty, truth, integrity, power, holy boldness, business, productivity and cultivation in His sons *(position, no gender)*. The Kingdom Mind the upgrade from the nature of man, authority, election, predestination, dominion, righteous anger, holiness, prosperity, ownership, identity and destiny. The role of the **Kingdom Mind** is to establish the Kingdom on earth as it is in heaven under the rule of King Jesus; manifesting the Kingdom of GOD, by sowing, initiating and reproducing heavenly affections and motives into the believer's new spirit for demonstration.

We must allow GOD access into our head. If the head is destroyed the body will die; spiritually and physically. The MIND-SPIRIT and the BODY have chemistry! Have you noticed the body follows and demonstrates the mind; the head that is leading? The body expresses the language of the mind. If the mind is empty the body will reflect emptiness. If the mind is idle or hostile the body behavior will reflect idleness or hostility. If the mind is corrupted the body will reflect corruption. If the mind is knowledgeable the body will reflect wisdom. If the mind is healed the body will reflect restoration. If the mind is under the influence of the Holy Spirit the body will reflect its character and wisdom. If the mind is baffled the body may reflect tension. Who's leading the universe of your mind? Our thoughts occupy shared portions of the brain. Our thoughts are the power that dictates to our point of view, behavior, what we do or do not believe, character and disposition. Our minds absorb even when we're not aware they are absorbing information. Our minds are very powerful tools of force and should be directed under the wisdom scope of Holy Spirit. *The Word of GOD declares in Isaiah 55:8 For my thoughts are not your thoughts, neither are your ways my ways.* As the LORD thoughts which are His Logos go out it will not return to Him empty *{Isaiah 55:11}.* When your mind is transformed then your atmosphere will change and the body will become subject to the leading of the new mind. It is the thoughts of GOD that conform our minds and behavior to His way, leaning not to our carnal understanding and acknowledging Him brings promise and promotion *{Proverbs 3:5-6}.* Whatever is the appetite of the mindset is what will give direction to a person's destiny. When Holy Spirit gets a grip of the mind, the head, and its creativity He restores the mind back to its Eden estate through the process of uprooting and planting and recreating the will. Holy Spirit doesn't retain the mind in its poverty or poor condition, but He resuscitates, elevates and cultivates it gradually to new heights and new dimensions in the image of GOD making it a universe of fruitfulness and a well-watered territory. *The Word of GOD declares in Philippians 2:5 Let this mind be in you, which was also in Christ Jesus.* Our job is to humble self and comply in faith. The DNA of the Spirit of Life mind is set above the elements of the world, powers, authorities, rulers, thrones and the courts in the cosmic; seen and unseen spheres. However, there is a war, a struggle between the flesh and the Spirit way of thinking and leading. The diabolic agenda that appeared as friend-friendly in Eden objective was to obtain **possession-ship, dominion-ship, loyalty-ship** and **position-ship**. Let's make it personal; one-on-one. There is a saying, you are what you eat. The spiritual saying is what has been sown by seed, placed in the ground *(soil)* of your heart and mind will become visible sooner or later through actions or conversation. The Word of GOD -Logos- Yeshua is a discerner of the intents of the heart *(mind)*. The Spirit of Life examines and proves the reigns, the minds of men. He examines the heart, spirit and mind of souls. He longs for **Lordship**, not just Savior; Lord of the harvest.

- *The Word of GOD declares in Hebrews 4:12 {Holman} The Word of God is living and effective and sharper than any double-edged sword, penetrating as far as the separation of the soul and spirit, joints and marrow. It is able to judge the ideas and thoughts of the heart.*

- *The Word of GOD declares in 1 Peter 4:1-2 Therefore, since Christ has suffered in the flesh, arm yourselves also with the same purpose, because he who has suffered in the flesh has ceased from sin, so as to live the rest of the time in the flesh no longer for the lusts of men, but for the will of God.*

- *The Word of GOD declares in Philippians 4:8 Finally brethren, whatsoever things are true, whatsoever things are honest, whatsoever things are just, whatsoever things pure, whatsoever things are of a good report: if there be any virtue, and if there be any praise, think on these things.*

These three powerful verses point to the activity of the brain and the activity of the heart; both serve output and input chemistry that causes reaction. Our thinking contributes to how we communicate, perceive things, handle situations, perform, relate to others and act on the Word. The mind can be viewed as being the power over the brain with its many compartments of division. We view the heart in relation to our sensitivity, but within the brain communicates the sensory characteristics such as: feelings, emotions, reasoning, pain, thoughts, visions, motives and imaginations which all points to the realm of the soul, the image of the heart *(see chapter 4, illustration B)*. If the brain stops working the body will be lifeless. If the heart stops beating the body will also be without life. Therefore, what we think very well transmits a great deal of our life's outcome. Yahweh-Elohim in all of His greatness knew what the cost of the fall would do to mankind soul and ability to function spiritually when the forbidden fruit in life was *(is)* eaten. Mankind is the only creature created with this capacity of power. The mind can be viewed as a pyramidal tier of unlimited powers. These powers are called conscious power, subconscious power and the unconscious power. A study shows that these powers make up a percentage of our thinking and related behavior. The illustration on the next page shows the conscious mind percentage at the top of the pyramidal triangle where communication, reasoning, daily thought and awareness takes place. The middle chamber of chambers communicates involuntarily relation to thoughts such as: repressed issues, feelings, emotions, dreams, spiritual, heartbeat and breathing and is connected to the unconscious mind system. And the lower chamber shows the unconscious mind or the mind that isn't aware, but functioning. This chamber of chambers transacts as a storehouse for all other chambers in the universe of the mind. Remember, the mind is spirit which is immaterial.

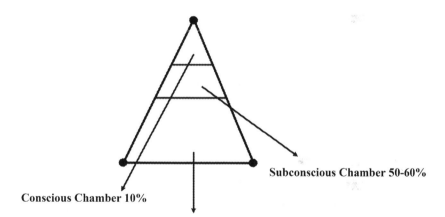

Subconscious Chamber 50-60%

Conscious Chamber 10%

Unconscious Chamber 30-40%

Greek term for Psychology
Psyche: mind, logos meaning knowledge or study of
Greek term for Soul
Psuche: breathe, blow, the soul
Hebrew term for Soul
Nephesh: a soul, living being, spirit, life

I hope you can see the connections from the spiritual side to the physical concerning the universe of the mind. If a person visits a Psychologist, the Psychologist will perform the study of the mind *(not the heart)* and related behavior due from chemical imbalances and possibly treat with therapy or medicine. Matters of the heart are matters of the mind can begin the process of healing through surgery of the soul. Taking the right prescription and dosage is vital to restoration.

- *The Word of GOD declares in Exodus 15:26 {AMP} Yahweh saying, if you diligently listen and pay attention to the voice of the LORD your GOD, and do what is right in His sight, and listen to His commandments, and keep (foremost in your thoughts and actively obey) all His percepts and statutes, then I will not put on you any of the diseases which I have put on the Egyptians: for I am the LORD who heals you.*

GOD is our healer, mind regulator and the great physician. He is Omnipotent, Omnipresent and Omniscience! He puts the Omni, ALL in all, that has been given in measure through technology and knowledge to earthly doctors; a measure of Himself. GOD has His way of revealing Himself to the Church through His prescribed Supernatural method. Just as doctors go to school, GOD takes His chosen to the School of the Holy Ghost for divine teaching and revelation deposit. We must learn to cultivate our hearing, our focus and our actions by the instructions of GOD through obedience! This is important to every believer's development after receiving the gift of salvation; now the road of sanctification life long process. After we hear, then we must hearken to the sober teaching instructions of the Ruach Hakodesh who will keep believers in perfect peace whose mind is stayed on Him *{Isaiah 26:3}*, because we trusted in Him. When your mind is stayed on Him it's a shift upwardly out from the natural carnal mindset. That means when the sheep rear off, he will be guided to return by the Shepherd's rod of vision, guidance and chastening. The carnal mind thinking and the supernatural mind thinking are on two different atmospheric frequencies similar to the location of the two trees in the Garden of Eden. Love, obedience and trust works like a cord of three strands that is not easily broken; yet woven together with supernatural strength and supernatural resistance. Jehovah Rapha is the great spiritual and physical physician who heals, cures, mends, repairs and makes whole the mind, the spirit, the body and the circumstance which helps the heart to function properly *{John 5:1-9; John 20:30-31}*.

Prayer

Heavenly Father, In the Name of Yeshua, I Thank You for Triumphant Dominion that Comes from You. There is None like You, LORD! You are Greatly to be Praised and Adored! I Honor and Magnify your Holy, Righteous and Majestic Name! Thank You for Making Me Whole. I Love You LORD! I Decree My Wealth Transfer to be Manifested in the Now in Yeshua's Name. I Decree a Supernatural Acceleration of Self-Control, Unconditional Love, Divine Peace, Divine Wisdom, Understanding, Spiritual Hunger and Spiritual Maturity Fill My Temple. I Decree a Supernatural Acceleration in my Income and Anointing in Yeshua's Name. Thank You LORD for Security and True Prosperity!

Amen.

Believers are supernaturally clothed in several divine gifts for divine purpose by Holy Spirit by putting on the **Kingdom-Mind of Christ**. These gifts work effectively by the will of the Spirit not by the will of the flesh. These gifts serve like a hard drive for the communication of the thoughts of Yahweh which are immeasurable. The seven-fold ministry of Yahweh unveils to believing believers ABBA's -thought- through His Ruach *(Spirit, wind, breathe)* from the **Mind of Christ**. The number seven *(physical and spiritual)* symbolically communicates GOD thoughts of divine wholeness, fullness, completeness and perfection in the spiritual and natural realm. Therefore, through the Mind of King JESUS a believer experiences a state of fullness by the Word of GOD. The LORD is connected directly *(indirectly)* to His creation. The **Mind of Christ** masters any challenges, any temptations, setbacks, fears, failures, lack, anxiety and weaknesses of the carnal mind through submission. When the revelation of whose you are in Christ is awaken, worries, troubles or sin will not easily conquer you or hold you hostage. The **Mind of Christ** functions to shift you into its principles of action causing you to respond from that dimension.

The first gift of the seven-fold ministry is the Spirit of the LORD. All things that are given of the Father to believers are done by the work of the Spirit of the LORD. And it is the same wind that He breathes to recreate. He breathes freshness into our human spirit and makes it alive. The Spirit of the LORD is the supernatural authority -source- that creates God's thoughts in our minds, opens our ears and eyes through agreement. The Spirit of the LORD dwells within the human spirit and rests upon believer's to do greater works. The Spirit of the LORD will not dwell in an unclean temple. The body of each believer is the temple of Holy Spirit *{2 Corinthians 6:16-18; 1 Corinthians 6:19}*. The Spirit of the LORD is the power source for the new spiritual building. The Spirit of the LORD is the divine Presence. "GOD is Spirit and His Spirit Breathes Continuous Life."

The second of the seven-fold ministry is the Spirit of Wisdom. The Spirit of Wisdom is divine wisdom completely different from earthly and human wisdom. God's divine wisdom makes one wise. *The Word of GOD declares in James 1:5 If any of you lack wisdom, let him ask of GOD.* This divine wisdom has nothing to do with age or gray hair or job position, education or how many degrees one may have or not, but it has everything to do with the one who supplies the inheritance benefits. The new spiritual house is furnished, built, established and sustained by the Spirit of Wisdom *{Proverbs 24:3}*. Divine wisdom is all of God's supernatural thoughts, plans and purposes. Wisdom instructs our path in the way of the Truth. The Spirit of the LORD instructs through the Spirit of Wisdom that man cannot live by bread alone, but by every word that proceeds out of the mouth of GOD *{Matthew 4:4}*. The Spirit of Wisdom is like a crown of grace to the head and truth around the neck *{Proverbs 1:9}*. The new birth is yoked to wisdom's guidance and without the yoke one will walk foolishly. It's an honorable place to be yoked to Yeshua who gives instructions pertaining to one's abundant life in the Kingdom of Yahweh *{Matthew 11:29}*. When the mind is yoked with the Spirit of the LORD, wisdom teaches one how to live as **one** and not walk contrary to the will of GOD presumptuously. He will not force anyone against their will. The Spirit of wisdom has drawn a divine line for each one to choose. Remember, there is power and influence in agreement.

The third of the seven-fold is the Spirit of Understanding which is God's illumination overshadowing the believer to bring insight of the wisdom that has been received. In order for us to understand and walk in what He reveals to us our minds must be illuminated by the Light. And to gain understanding in areas where we lack understanding are illuminated also by the Light of Truth. The Light of illumination brings clarity and specific details. The Spirit of Understanding blocks out barrenness, confusion, delusion and illusion; and produces evidence of fruitfulness in ones life when the mind is renewed. *The Word of GOD declares in Proverbs 3:5-6 Trust in the Lord with all thine heart; and lean not unto thine own understanding. In all thy ways acknowledge Him and He shall direct thy paths.* A lack of understanding can lead to anxiousness, misunderstanding, arguments, fights, discord, doubt, paths that are not directed by the Lord and unwanted open doors. Unwanted doors if not closed can lead to other territories that will lead ones heart out of the will of GOD. Developing good judgment and good insight have there reward when we lean not to our own understanding. Yet to develop that wisdom the Mind of Christ must be put on. The Spirit of wisdom and understanding divinely works together as one power *{Proverbs 4:5-7}.*

The fourth of the seven-fold is the Spirit of Counsel; knowing what GOD has to say or what He is saying about life matters should be of concern to each believer. The Spirit of Counsel is like an advisor cautioning us on what is or isn't the best course of action or what is or isn't the will of the Father. The Spirit of Counsel releases its knowledge through us to pour into others, as well as, into ourselves the virtue of Christ. The Spirit of Counsel delegate's sober judgment, discernment in matters, brings correction, peace, reconciliation, direction, assurance and also hostility from mindsets that are unequally yoked, walking in denial or compromising. The Spirit of Counsel is like supernatural therapy from GOD to guide believers in making wise decisions. It should be practical to seek God's counsel regarding every area of one's life. It's a wise decision to seek His counsel prior to making decisions that may go wrong or not be good for your present or future state. However, this is how many of us learn. Therefore, as we learn we should take heed to seeking His way first to avoid the pit holes that lie ahead. The decisions a person makes can affect them long term and affect those closely associated. Its wise to seek His counsel first for a soul mate, what neighborhood to move in, job relocations, seasons during the lose of a love one, where to open a business, how to parent your children, how to love, how to continue in marriage after difficult experiences, what to do during a crisis, what's next after a divorce, practicing abstinence until marriage or what college to attend. Those are just a few ideas that need the help from the Spirit of Counsel. List others that are revealed concerning you and take them before the LORD your Counselor.

The fifth of the seven-fold ministry is the Spirit of Might. The Spirit of Might speaks of God's supernatural ability to perform His thoughts through earthly vessels which in our human strength we could not perform. The Mind of Christ confirms that in Him we can master what is before us; it is within us from the Master, Adonai. All that Holy Spirit owns is invested in the heirs of Christ who are spiritual beings. Remember, the Spirit of the Lord's Might puts the supernatural upon, as well as, within us. This supernatural ability is called the anointing. Yahweh's might is unchangeable. The Spirit of Might is like a giant that stands tall in the believer making one immovable and unstoppable through the power of the Spirit of the LORD. This is the authority of the **Kingdom-Mind of Christ** that causes us not to waver, but to become flint in the Spirit against resistance to the way of Light. Casting out devils, speaking with new tongues, healing the sick, laying hands *{Acts 10:38}*, living holy, loving the unlovable and forgiving the unforgivable are works of the Spirit of Might working through open hearts and minds. It's through the Spirit of Might that the Church declares war on anything that attempts to hold us down through the expression of the living WORD of GOD. *The Word of GOD declares in Isaiah 61 The Spirit of the LORD is upon me because the Lord has anointed me to preach the gospel to the poor, recovery of sight to the blind, to bind up the broken hearted and to proclaim freedom to the captives.* Whenever there is resistance in the realm of the spirit and limitation in our human strength the believer is authorized and deputized to display the manifold wisdom of GOD; supernatural authority of the Spirit of Might *{Ephesians 3:10}*. It is not by our strength, nor by our power or might, but by the Spirit of the LORD of host *{Zechariah 4:6}*. Trials rise to stir us to stir up the gifts within our new nature. Think about that. GOD will use and allow issues to come in the physical realm to usher the believer into the supernatural realm for spiritual warfare, relocation, transformation and transition. The Body of Christ is the mandated institution of authority, power and demonstration from heaven to the earth by the Government of GOD in Christ. **"I Prophesy to You That You Are the Change For the Change, Take Your Dominion."** Samson, Elijah and Paul are three along with others who demonstrated the Spirit of Might through the power of the Mighty One *{Psalms 50:1-2; Ephesians 2:6}*.

The sixth gift of the seven-fold ministry is the Spirit of Knowledge. We all need divine knowledge which counteracts ignorance and supersedes our conscious mind. The Spirit of Knowledge is the utterance of unknown knowledge that you wasn't aware of mentally. Remember, knowledge is the power of influence that is powerful and without it we perish; in thought and in deed. This foreknowledge of GOD overrides head knowledge and comes from a deep living experience that has been birth forth in the mind and floods the soul with deftness of the revelation of GOD the Father. The Spirit of Knowledge is seeing, hearing and receiving God's thoughts manifested in our life through exploits and exposure. The Spirit of Knowledge takes your new mind to the dimension of its reality in faith and of power. The Spirit of Knowledge will empower the believer not to go backwards, because of the supernatural revelation obtained through experiential encounter that is now a priceless and rewarding possession. The Spirit of Knowledge will also bring holy conviction. *The Word of GOD declares in Daniel 11:32 {NIV} With flattery he will corrupt those who have violated the covenant, But the people who know their GOD will firmly resist him and do exploits.* Divine knowledge reveals divine revelation. The Spirit of Knowledge DNA impresses a hope of certainty within the spirit -mind- that there is no turning back now know matter what comes.

- *The Word of GOD declares in Proverbs 1:7 The fear of the LORD is the beginning of knowledge but fools despise wisdom and instruction.*

The last of the seven-fold ministry is the Spirit of the fear of the LORD which is healthy and rich attribute. When believers truly walk in God's tender mercy, loving kindness, commands and in His truth toward others and toward Him this is evident of the Spirit of the fear of the LORD. Remember, how we treat others is a reflection of the character and Spirit of Yahweh. We are created in His image. DNA approved! The Spirit of the fear of the LORD is demonstrated by walking *(abiding)* in God's love and truth through the influential power of the Holy Spirit; consciously fleeing anything that would quench His Spirit and mar our spirit. The Spirit of the fear of the LORD causes His enemies to flee Him and His elect to run to the name of the LORD. The awakening divine knowledge of the Spirit of the LORD brings us to this dimension. The greater our love and understanding is for GOD the greater our fear *(respect, awesome reverence)* for Him will be. The Spirit of the fear of the LORD is surrounded by the revelation of His love, compassion, jealousy, deliverance and faithfulness that is revealed toward His chosen. This Ruach Hakodesh *(Holy Spirit)* develops sensitivity in the heart of believing believers of the awesomeness of Almighty GOD and keeps us from sinning *{Exodus 20:18-20}*. A lack of spiritual sensitivity to the manifested power of GOD can be a result from the lack of the sensitivity to the Holy Spirit in ones heart. This also can be applied to the whole of the seven-fold ministry of the Spirit of the LORD. Spiritual sensitivity is vital for responsiveness, accountability and maturity. As the redeemed of the Lord, we should thirst for more of the outpouring of the seven-fold ministry to be evident in our lives as new creatures. The Spirit of the LORD through the **Mind of Christ** brings all these wealthy riches to function within the sons of GOD *{Isaiah 11:2}*. We are destined through the plan of GOD to be triumphant in Christ not sometimes, but every time as we humble ourselves, yield and seek Him. The King has given the citizens of the Kingdom true riches that will never fail or forsake us; yet is profitable to us. The gifts contain principles that are to be deposited, processed and applied to our renewed mind and renewed soul. This seven-fold ministry of Ruach HaKodesh *(Holy Spirit)* is the manifestations of the attributes of Yahweh-Elohim and the believer's revealed traits in Christ. By the wisdom of the Spirit we understand that the image of GOD and His glory isn't placed on the physical appearance of what Adam or what we actually look like outwardly, but rather on the inward **substance** and **ability to function** under the **canopy of Light** projecting the Creator's divine image and thought.

- *The Word of GOD declares in 1 Corinthians 2:14-16 But a natural man does not accept the things of the Spirit of God, for they are foolishness to him; and he cannot understand them, because they are spiritually appraised. But he who is spiritual appraises all things, yet he himself is appraised by no one. For who hath known the mind of the Lord, that he may instruct Him? But we have the mind of Christ.*

- *The Word of GOD declares in John 16:12-15 I have many more things to say to you, but you cannot bear them now. But when He, the Spirit of Truth comes, He will guide you into all truth; for He will not speak on His own initiative, but whatever He hears, He will speak; and He will disclose it to you. All things that the Father has are Mine; therefore, I said that He takes of Mine and will disclose it to you.*

The Kingdom Mind is accelerated by the Ruach during times of pure intimacy, praise, worship and living a life that is being laid prostrate in the Presence of GOD. That means there is a constant dying of the mind of your flesh and a spiritual appetite that is increasing in the blessings of GOD. GOD the Holy Spirit will speak His thoughts to us while driving, in the tub, times of meditation, cooking, asleep and especially when we still ourselves from busyness. GOD can speak to you at anytime and in whatever way He chooses. When our souls are open to receive the **Mind of Christ** will flow. These blessings flow beyond material contentment. These are supernatural blessings of the spiritual flow that can impact change in the lives of others. These are blessings that cause the devil to flee when you open your mouth from a sincere heart to praise GOD and/ or pray. These are powerful blessings that command blessings that are held up in the heavens to be released and manifested in the earth realm. These are blessings when you're about to lose your mind and the Spirit fullness covers your nakedness with meekness. It's nice to have material things, but it's greater to have the **Mind of Christ** activated to help keep or maintain what you already have been blessed to receive or about to receive or *even to lose.* Sometimes GOD will allow stuff to be removed out of our atmosphere because of where we are or how we are or what we are lacking from Him. Selah! Adam and Eve were shown the exit out of the Garden of Eden, but the sons of GOD *(children led of the Spirit of God)* have been shown by the Spirit how to enter into His Presence. It's your season to shift through the Kingdom Mind of speaking what heaven is speaking about that which concerns your Eden. In ABBA's Presence is where we find the treasure of wealth. If you want your heart filled, I beseech you to get into His Presence. ABBA loves to flow His mind through any soul that will sellout to Him by becoming a living sacrifice, pure and holy laying aside all foolishness. It's time to rise up and walk in dominion. We walk imperfectly in the flesh, but Yahweh commands the believers to walk before Him and be thou perfect *{Genesis 17:1}*. We cannot accomplish this blameless or mature walk in the mind of the flesh only through the mind of the Spirit of Christ. When the Ruach permeates words of instruction into your heart you have a choice to obey or disobey. Now, the scriptures clearly tell the Ekklesia that we do not belong to ourselves any longer, for we have been bought with the rich price of pure royal blood. This is another reason why the Kingdom Mind is given to every believer for the purpose of overcoming self. Yes, self-will is our greatest enemy. Yahweh the Father desires that the Church become **ONE** with His mind, not the other way around. When we understand our DNA we do not fight the same way as the world or when we walked the way of worldliness. We activate the dominant **Mind of Christ**.

It is the **Mind of Christ** that prevents the soul from conforming to the genetic patterns or elements in this worldly system. It is the **Mind of Christ** that empowers through heaven's frequency how to discern the good and perfect will of GOD. The gift is imparted by the

GOD-gene and when activated it makes known the GOD universe of revelation that surpass life as we once knew it. The mind is the seat of awareness, decisions, intellect and reasoning. The mind can be viewed as having two major switches; a good switch and a bad switch or a positive or negative switch, new switch or old switch, a switch that has power to restore and the other switch that has power to destroy. Remember, as stated before, the mind is a spiritual force connected to the spirit world. Thoughts and influences enter in and exit out without your permission. However, for believers in Christ we have been given authorization through the ***Kingdom*-Mind of Christ** to change the climate in that atmospheric territory. We have power and authority over what goes and what remains. This is the dominion of cultivating our garden. ***The Word of GOD declares in 2 Corinthians 10:5 Casting down imaginations, and every high thing that exalt itself against the knowledge of God, and bringing into captivity every thought to the obedience of Christ.*** There is nothing that is in the unseen realm or seen realm of the universe or in the universe of your soul -mind- that He is not knowledgeable of. The DNA GOD-gene carries and embeds the Mind of Yeshua HaMashiach which reveals the hidden things of the Kingdom of GOD to His elect as He wills. This new mind will be challenged by the old switch of reasoning and attitudes derived from the old sinful nature. The new language of the new mind cannot flow from the old nature. Therefore, we must consistently renew our mind with the wealth of the WORD of GOD. As we stay the course according to the way of the leading of Holy Spirit and not the will of the mind of the flesh, we will see the manifestations of victory that has already been predestined before the foundation of the world in Christ. The **Mind of Christ** promotes acceleration in the new renewed spirit of man by the language of heaven. The WORD of GOD likened to grain produces fattening in the Spirit. The flesh cannot produce this governing fruitful work of the Spirit.

- ***The Word of GOD declares in Romans 7:18 For I know that in me (that is my flesh) dwells no good thing: for to will is present with me; but how to perform that good I find not.***

As Apostle Peter warns us this world is not the children of GOD home *{1 Peter 2:11-12}*; therefore, we are not to conform to its ideology and idolatrous ways, but be transformed by the renewing of our mind and conforming to the Holy Spirit *{Romans 12:1-2}*. We must die to the old way of thinking by putting off the old self and its former manner of life *{Ephesians 2:22-24}*. Apostle Paul testifies that nothing righteous or good lives in the mind of the flesh, for the law of sin and death dwells in the body *{Romans 7:14-25}*. The governing mind of the flesh is the state of the unrestrained desires, passions, appetite, ignorance, reasoning and consciousness of the soul without the influential power of the Holy Spirit working within. The spirit, soul and mind can only be renewed by the power of the Holy Spirit through yielding to the new supernatural mind switch. The temple has to be supernaturally swept for habitation by the Law of the Spirit; redemption and sanctification. GOD wants your body, too! This takes place when your mind is in agreement with the control of the new mind. This allows the Holy Spirit to run freely; effectively opposing the resistance that rise inwardly giving us supernatural power to resist and overcome fleshly inclinations of gratifying the unwholesome deeds of the flesh. As you earnestly desire the meat of the Word, cleave to the Truth and RESIST the unfruitful cravings of the sinful nature the manifestations of the **Mind of Christ** are bounded to rise inwardly in divine strength. The meat of the Word brings about effectiveness and stoutheartedness in the power of the Lord. As we mature in the Lord, we should not be continually stumbling over the same sins or temptations or weaknesses or weights. That is a sign of stubbornness and rejection toward the **WORD of GOD** that leads to hardness of heart. The consequences are not favorable, but extremely deadly. In spite of there appearing, battle in victory, according to His Word. Believer's lives are to show evidence of the worthiness of the calling and the Glory of GOD. We may get knocked back, but never to the place of No come back in Christ. GOD is the sower of His Word, Holy Spirit breathes on His Word for heart and mind absorption and swells the knowledge and wisdom in the heart to erase the old mind switch and its desires; giving entrance for all that pertains to the new mind frequency with its new desires and affections from heaven.

- *The Word of GOD declares to the elect in Hebrew 10:31 {AMP} It is a fearful thing to fall into the hands of the Living GOD (incurring His judgment and wrath).*

- *The Word of GOD cautions the elect in Philippians 2:12b Walk out thy own salvation in fear and trembling.*

The word spirit also denotes character. When the LORD builds His spiritual building it's through His blueprint only. Kingdom character is instilled in the spiritual building for God's workmanship to display through us. The blueprint is filled with Holy Spirit for the proper expansion of the heart, the mind, the spirit and the body and how it conducts its members. The Spirit has the complete plan for the construction of all the members of the new building. The body complies with the head that's leading the new mind site. As the spiritual building is properly being built it is structured only by the mind of Christ to withstand changes, droughts and temptations that will come in their seasons *{Colossians 3:2-10}*. The spiritual building increases in its declared worth, stability and assurance instead of decreasing in property value because of the new mind renovations and alterations. The changes that are unfavorable to us are dealt with through self examination, prayer and submission. The plan of GOD is fixed and built on the solid Rock of Truth *{Matthew 7:24-27}*. The spirit of compromise, lukewarmness and mixture can cause the building to cave in, decay and fall *{Romans 6:13}*. We as believers are Glory carriers through Christ and the new building stamped by the Spirit's approval displays the Glory of the LORD. Our resurrected hearts and minds bear the Light of Christ that is to shine forth the Glory of GOD. *The Word of GOD declares in Romans 8:9 However, you are not in the flesh but in the Spirit, if indeed the Spirit of God dwells in you, But if anyone does not have the Spirit of Christ, he does not belong to Him.* GOD always moves in the era of the **new** *{Isaiah 43:18-19; 42:9}*. It's His Nature to Do New Things! The heart, the spirit and the tongue must come into alignment with the Mind of Christ. **Shift!** You are a new creation, made new and the old has passed way.

- *The Word of GOD declares in 2 Corinthians 5:17 If any man be in Christ, he is a new creature: old things are passed away; behold, all things are become new.*

- *The Word of GOD declares in Romans 12:2 And be not conformed to this world; but be transformed by the renewing of the mind that ye may prove what is that good and acceptable and perfect will of GOD.*

When ungodly or vain thoughts rise out of the past by way of the old mind switch through an open door in your soul, cast it down with your new mind language. There is supernatural power in you to push back the enemy of your soul. The old has know hold on the new; it is powerless to hold you. However, a hold comes from the cord of agreement; if that is the case it is in violation of the **Mind of Christ Constitutional Rights** and most be severed in JESUS Name. You must fall out of agreement with vain imaginations. Oftentimes, things can lay dormant in a soul until a situation arises and flares up the unhealed soul. However, I know ABBA wants you to hear and reflect what His thoughts have already declared, so you can approach the circumstance with your new language from being born from above. Although challenges or tests may come to prove us, we must apply Kingdom laws, Kingdom mindset and prayer of deliverance *(putting self on the altar)* to render self out of the way; then to the circumstance by sending forth the Word into the atmosphere. But we must get ourselves out of the way so that the Word can impact the circumstances and closure can take place. Time is now to rise up from that place and meet Him by switching off the old paradigm and operating in the **Kingdom-Mind of Christ** paradigm. Just as Adam *(Eve)* was commanded to dominate in paradise and cultivate all that was in his care, we are charged to do the same with all that is in our care through the provision of the mind of Christ. Our new location places us in partnership with Christ; recognizing and keeping intruders out of our garden.

GOD is not mocked. No one who dishonors the WORD of GOD as if there is not a penalty to be paid or if the law doesn't apply to all gets away. He cannot be deceived by cunningness or craftiness or cleverness by the old nature's mindset. It is ordained by Yahweh that all souls will reap what one has sown in due season *{Galatians 6:7-8}* our due measure. The heart and mind lay transparent before the eyes of GOD who is Holy. Things on this side may seem as if there is no record being kept, but there is heavenly book of records; and GOD who is compassionate and longsuffering wills that sinning hearts **repent**. No one escapes or gets away from the justice system of the divine courtroom of Yahweh GOD. All matters of the heart and deeds carried out in the flesh are and will be judged. It is revealed in Eden with the account that sin doesn't go unpunished. A criminal may seem as if they have gotten away from authorities and there is no penalty for the crimes that were committed. However, there is a day of reckoning, for all souls and all flesh that is approaching at its appointed time. *The Word of GOD declares in Proverbs 14:12 There is away that seemly appears or looks right unto man, but in the end it leads to death.*

The **Mind of Christ** is the governing mind that possesses the Kingdom of God's fortified estate. The **Mind of Christ** has a spiritual radar sensor for the equipping of the saints. Because there are numerous dimensions in heaven, the estate is accessed through the mind of the rich. JESUS became poor that we may become rich and receive the riches of His Kingdom through Holy Spirit. There are riches that He has loosed to us, yet have not manifested. The **Mind of Christ** commands that all blockages due to the lack of knowledge, worth, self-will, excuses, deep hurt and lack of commitment unto Him "Be Gone, Broken Off of Your Life!" Yeshua wants all of you, not just the portion you give of yourself to Him. If there are any doors that you have not given Him access to He is calling out to you today; the time is now to remove the restrictions. Since, The LORD is our Strong Tower and our Fortress listed below are powerful gifts that He has authorized though the **Mind of Christ** for Kingdom manifestations and demonstrations of the divine nature in this foreign land. GOD the Holy Spirit equips the warring bride with all she needs to obtain victory. He imparts the reality of the Kingdom through Himself:

- Indwelling of Holy Spirit!
- Divine Planting!
- Divine Revelation!
- Divine Wisdom!
- Divine Knowledge!
- Divine Strength!
- Divine Crowns!
- Divine Access!
- Divine Resurrection Power!
- Divine Transformation!
- Divine Seeing!
- Divine Hearing!
- Divine Encounters!

The prayers of the upright in heart avail much since they are prayers released out of the **Kingdom-Mind of Christ**. Is there anything too hard for GOD? NO! There is nothing too hard for GOD! Therefore, your new spirit releases the identity charges "I Can Do All Things through Christ who Strengthens me" and "With GOD All Things Are Possible to me." A present place that seems limited in your eyes doesn't determine God's thoughts or plans. However, His thought –WORD –SEED determines your destiny in Him as you trust and obey. The Sword swings both ways.

Shift! Keep on praying, keep on seeking and keep on decreeing the shift in the Spirit by the Spirit. The Wisdom of GOD is great above all human knowledge and understanding and creation itself. The Ekklesia's full and complete identity in Christ provides all that is needed to conquer, rule, reign, overcome and walk in harmony in this world. Yahweh-Elohim will continue to fill the temple with the new Wine as self is being sacrificed. Don't run or dismiss the process or probation period that is allowed to teach you how to war against your flesh and throw off the cares of this world in the supernatural and in the natural realm. We are winners through the **DNA of the Word, the Blood and the Spirit.** The Spirit, the Water and the Blood are in agreement supernaturally bearing witness in the earth as **One** *{1 John 5:8}*. Make your confession: **I Am ONE with the MIND of Christ Jesus!**

The Supernatural DNA sets the Bride of Christ apart from the ways of the mind system of this world and connects us with the ways of the Kingdom of Yahweh-Elohim. You are His prized possession. Because our divine nature- identity is in Christ, we have been equipped to cross over into the realm of the spirit in the Holy

Spirit through the **Kingdom Mind** under an open heaven to untie, release blessings, prophesy and remove blockages, live in victory and decree the promises of the Promise; receiving the wealth transfer and impartation. Pray and seek GOD for His double portion and be **Ready** to stand against opposition being cloaked in the authority of the MIND of Christ. Heavenly Father you said, it pleases you to see your children prosper. Release your double Father for your glory in Yeshua's *(Jesus)* name.

- Divine Anointing!
- Divine Increase!
- Divine River Flow!
- Divine Restoration!
- Divine Healing!
- Divine Awakening
- Divine Protection!
- Divine Mind!
- Divine Finance Release!
- Divine Connection!
- Divine Peace!
- Divine Love!
- Divine Health!
- Divine Substance!
- Divine Shift!
- Divine Sound!
- Divine Appointment!
- Divine Elevation!
- Divine Timing!

NOTES:

_____

_____

_____

_____

_____

_____

_____

_____

_____

_____

_____

_____

_____

_____

_____

_____

_____

_____

_____

_____

_____

_____

_____

_____

_____

_____

_____

_____

Study Review:

1. Whose image are you created in and how? Explain.

    _____

    _____

    _____

2. Define Identity in Christ?

    _____.

    a) Who defines that origin, Christ or the world? _____.
    b) How? _____.

3. Who purchased you with Blood, True Riches, Purity and Glory? _____.
    a) What does his name means in Hebrew? _____.
    b) Explain the blood antidote with two supporting verses of scripture.

    _____

    _____

    _____

4. How does the Blood of Jesus cleanse you and remove the guilt?

    _____

    _____

    _____

5. How has Yeshua re-established your birthright with benefits and a future? _____.

   a) Explain your answer with scripture

_____

_____

_____

6. How does the mind and heart functions relate to each other?

_____

_____

_____

7. Are you in right standing with Yahweh according to His Court of Law? _____.

8. What word does the Holy Bible not man define as right standing?

_____

_____

9. What does the phrase "In Christ" determines to believers?

_____

_____

10. What is the Glory? _____

   a) Write 4 verse references and explain them.

_____

_____

_____

_____

11. How does Seed function?

_____

_____

12. What does Seed mean?

_____

_____

13. What does having the Mind of Christ accomplish? And what is the reward(s)?

_____

_____

_____

14. As believers how does the Mind of Christ function in our spirit?

_____

_____

15. Since the heart is the muscle organ that pumps blood to and from the heart how does the heart and mind spiritually and naturally relate to your renewed state of being?

_____

_____

16. What organ in the body demonstrates its character of action? Hint above. What is the scripture verse?

_____

_____

17. What is the old switch? How do the believers combat the old switch?

_____

_____

18. What have you as a believing believer been created to do through your new nature?

_____

19. Are you allowing your old nature to control? _____.

    a) If yes, what is Holy Spirit instructing you to do to overcome your strong will and self?

_____

_____

20. What does it mean to "guard" your heart?

_____

_____

_____

21. Who is the garden? _____. What is the soil? _____.

22. What does it mean to "cultivate" your garden?

_____

_____

23. What is the frequency of believer's new mind? _____.

24. What scripture verse provides the sevenfold ministry of the Spirit of GOD? _____.

25. Are you allowing the sevenfold ministry gifts to flow through you? _____.

26. Describe the Mind of Christ?

_____.

27. Name five characteristics of having the Mind of Christ that are to be active within and without:

- _____
- _____
- _____
- _____
- _____

28. Memorize Hebrews 11:1 _____

29. Memorize Romans 12:1-2

_____

_____

30. Describe the function of the mind of Christ and how it relates to the new birth (believers).

_____

_____

_____

31. What do you see in your bloodline that needs to be purged with by Blood of Yeshua and the Sword of the Spirit?

- _____
- _____
- _____

32. According to this study, what steps are believers to initiate to begin the deliverance process or to stand in the gap for others that may be bound?

- _____
- _____
- _____

GLOSSARY

Adam: man, mankind; form of the word adamah

Adamah: (Hebraic): earth, dust, ground: adom(red), admoni(ruddy) and dam(blood)

Advocate: Yeshua: redeemer's defense attorney who vindicates and represents the worshiper in the Divine Kingdom Courts before YHWH, God the Father

Affections: degenerated or generated inner parts; passions, emotions, lust

Apostasy: falling away, rejection, rebellious

Blemish: {greek word spilos} impure, guilty, a stain; outside of the will of GOD

Blood: life, natural source for the physical life

Bloodline: traces of ancestor lineage, parent, generational characteristics, spiritual gateway; inheritance

Carnal Mind: seat of thought, emotions, soulish, reasoning faculty, intellect, thinking, thoughts, fleshly, immaterial; supernatural, Christ mind, kingdom

Cell: the smallest structural unit pertaining to life that can replicate itself independently, called the building blocks of life

Charisma: compelling attractiveness, alluring, charming presence

Chromosomes: Greek-Chroma (color), Soma (body) patterns of light and dark; Tsadi root of Tumor- to sprout or grow up, to swell

Chronos: 24hrs, timing related to minutes and seconds

Code: a secret system of communication, principle, signals, symbols, letters, sounds, light, flashes and rules

Covenant: {hebrew word b'rit, greek word diatheke} divine bond, a will, a testament; a binding constitution of benefits given by one party to another; agreement between two parties, YHWH (Jehovah) and man

Corrosion: gradual deterioration or destruction by force of the old nature

Darkness: absence of light, void, empty of moral and spiritual understanding, truth

Decode: interpretation, change or translation of a code

Defection: departure from Truth; corruption, defilement

Degenerated: declined spiritual condition, impure, spiritually dead, corrupt, fallen nature, not saved

Delusion: false belief maintained that contradicts truth, from inner feelings

Demoralize: to throw something into disorder, to destroy the confidence and hope of a person

Denounce: to personally abandon, expose or reject something publically

Desire: to yearn for or long after; delight in something

Dichotomous: as soul and body

Distort: misleading or false information; to pervert, twist, make crooked

Divine: the supernatural, relating to, coming from the Supreme-being

DNA: transmission of codes or genetic information, transcript; the molecule of life (according to dictionary.com noun-Biochemistry) is deoxyribonucleic acid: a self replicating material present in nearly all living organisms as the main constituent of chromosomes. It is a carry of genetic information that includes the plant kingdom and the animal kingdom.

Dormant: inactive state, a deep sleep; not growing, but have the ability to grow

Elohim / Elohyim: Creator and judge of the universe, plurality of the Godhead, plural hebrew translation title El {title-God, god, Eloah} Strong One

Encode: code predetermined and responsible for producing a substance or nature

Flint: firmness, not to shrink from any degree of suffering for the sake of accomplishing the work of Christ

Gene: basic physical unit of heredity; a linear sequence of nucleotides along a segment of DNA that provides the coded instructions for synthesis of RNA, when translated into protein leads to the expression of hereditary character {Dated 1911 Danish Geneticist}. The woven simplicity of the fabric thread of life

Genetics: the study of heredity or the variation of inherited generated characteristics. Every living thing contains the genetic codec that makes up DNA molecules. The codec cell is passed on when organisms reproduce. The basic unit of heredity is the gene which tells the body and the soul how to function, develop and respond.

Generate: create, (re)produce by a process, engender, provoke; to come about

Glory of God: {hebrew kavod} heaviness, weighty; manifestation of the presence and image of the invisible God

Holy Spirit: Spirit of God/ Spirit of Christ-Ruach Hakodesh {Hebraic} pronunciation ROO-akh Hah-koh-desh; governing authority and rule of the Kingdom of GOD

Indoctrinate: cause someone to believe a belief with the motive to pervert their thought without any choice of options

Inherent: built-in, hereditary; substance of the nature residing as the identity of that substance by nature legally as a right, a benefit and a privilege

Iniquity: wickedness, evil, twisted, perverted

Identity: the distinguished character or inner being of an individual, core of being

Illusion: misleading in thought, deception of the mind from outside influence

Image: {hebrew word Tselem, Demuth} shape, shadow, pattern, form, to be like, likeness, resemblance

In the flesh: sinful nature, affections and desires that are contrary or hostile to God through the body, soul and mind

In the Spirit: renewed affections and desires that under the influence of God's Spirit and mastered

Kairos: related to God seasons and appointed time, supreme moment

Kingdom: sphere, territory, realm subject to the governmental authority and power of a king over citizens

Light: {greek word phos} the source through Christ, manifestation of incarnate GOD; to make to see, evident, exposing and overcoming darkness, illumination to reveal and impart, bring forth

Marred: blemished, corruption of the soul

Mediator: the act of intervening between two opposing parties' man and YHWH the Father; negotiator or go-between establishing a peace-bond agreement, to put things right

Midst: there, mid, surrounded by, unknown, atmospheric

Mind of Christ: seat of divine reflection, transforming, illumination, supernatural, Yahweh's thought, will

Mocked: treat with contempt, laugh at, to disgrace, to dishonor

Mutation: the act of changing the nature within a thing or person, to alter

Nature: imprint, make up, origin of birth and growth

New Mind: divinely renewed reflection, inborn, from above, new nature's thought

Old Mind: hostile toward GOD, inner parts, sinful flesh, in the dark, weak, can't please the Father

Presence of God: {hebrew Panim translated face} a close and personal encounter with the Lord, the dwelling and settling of the presence of the LORD in the midst

Reciprocity: receiving and giving in return of that which was given

Renounce: reject, disown, no longer engage in

Retribution: a return; divine reward or divine punishment

Regenerated: reborn, new life in Christ Jesus; born again of the Spirit of Christ

Seed: {hebrew zera} offspring, starting of life {greek sperma} deposit

Seared Conscience: permanent altered, numbness in moral judgment of right and wrong

Sin: transgression against the law of God, shameful behavior in thought or deed that offends and opposes God

Sinister: forbidding; something evil or harmful that is or will happen

Shekinah Glory: dwelling, settling of the divine presence of God

Soulish: derived from the greek word psuchikos; mind {pusche-soul} of the fleshly nature which receive not the spiritual things of GOD; house emotions, the will, the mind, desires, carnal feelings, governed by the soul or the regenerated Spirit

Spirit: {hebrew ruach / greek pneuma} breathe, blow, wind, cool, strength, heart, mind, thoughts, authority of the immaterial nature and power of YHWH Elohyim; governs the soul and body

Technicality: detail information understood by someone with advance revelation/ skill

Transgression: violation of law, wrongdoing, disobedience

Transformation: divine change in the human nature, mind; alteration from within

Trichotomous: three parts-nature of man; spirit, soul and body

Tree of Life: {hebrew Etz Chayim} seed of righteousness, eternal life, immortality, counsel of wisdom; Yeshua is the Tree of Life

Tree of knowledge of good and evil: {hebrew Etz ha-da'at tov va-ra} seed of Satan, counsel of death and darkness

Universe: domain, sphere, world

Yeshua HaMashiach: {translation Jesus Christ-Messiah} the radiant glory of the Father, the exact representation of His nature, Son of GOD, Redeemer, Deliverer

YHVH: {Yod Heh Vaw Heh (Yahveh, Yahweh-hebrew} Eternal One, LORD God who keeps Covenant; to be, to cause to come to pass, self-existent

.

IN THE MIDST OF THE STORM THERE IS PURPOSE
BOOK ORDER INFORMATION

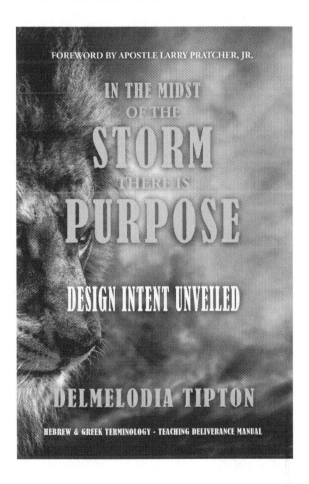

Available in three formats: softcover, hardcover, ebook

Amazon.com | Authorhouse.com

AMBASSADORS 4CHRIST APOSTOLIC BROADCAST
MINISTRY | www.ambassaduer4christ.net